ARCHITECTURAL PRACTICE:
THE SOUTH CAROLINA CHAPTER OF THE AMERICAN INSTITUTE OF ARCHITECTS

ARCHITECTURAL PRACTICE:
THE SOUTH CAROLINA CHAPTER OF THE AMERICAN INSTITUTE OF ARCHITECTS

John M. Bryan

"The South Carolina Chapter of the American Institute of Architects is unique, for it has worked as a group to improve the professional standards of architecture. It played an important role as the School of Architecture became an independent college within the framework of Clemson University and collaborated in the fund raising and establishment of off-campus programs in South Carolina and Europe. These projects have been vigorously supported by South Carolina architects in good times and bad, and this book covers the history of this period of dramatic change."

Harlan E. McClure, FAIA, 1916 - 2001
Dean Emeritus
College of Arts, Architecture & Humanities
Clemson University

AIA/SC History Book Task Force
James L. Thomas, Chairman
Phelps Bultman, Earle Gaulden, and Peter McKellar

Book Design and Photography
Hunter L. Clarkson, Alt Lee, Inc.

Layout and Design
Mary Lynn Fowler

Published in Columbia, South Carolina
by the AIA/SC

Copyright 2003 by John M. Bryan

Printed in China at Palace Press International

Library of Congress Card Number: 2003103044

First Edition, 2003

ISBN 0-9701267-2-7

Table of Contents

Acknowledgements vii

Preface xii

Forward
By Thompson E. Penney, FAIA xiii

Chapter One
History, c. 1735-1955..1

Chapter Two
Architectural Education in South Carolina, c. 1950-1981
By Harlan McClure, FAIA 53

Chapter Three
Significant Developments, c. 1963-2002 83

Honors, Awards and Rosters of Membership 98
    Honorary Members of the AIA from SC 98
    Honorary Affiliate Members - AIA/SC 104
    Medal of Distinction Recipients - AIA/SC 105
    Firm Awards - AIA/SC 106
    Alliance Award Recipients - AIA/SC 107
    Design Awards - AIA 108
    Design Awards - South Atlantic Region - AIA 110
    Design Awards - AIA/SC 112
    Robert Mills Residential Design Awards 154
    Officers and Regional Directors of the AIA from SC 160
    Past Presidents of the AIA/SC 161
    Fellows of the American Institute of Architects 164
    AIA Emeritus Members 166
    AIA Members..168
    Associate AIA Members 186
    Professional affiliate Members 191
    AIA/SC Staff 191

Bibliography 192

Acknowledgements

This book began as a gleam in the eye of James Lee Thomas, FAIA. In January 2000, he took me to lunch and presented his vision of an illustrated history of the architectural profession in South Carolina. Before I could form a list of excuses, he convened a group which became known as the History Book Task Force – Pete McKellar, AIA, representing the Lowcountry, Earle Gaulden, FAIA representing the Upstate, and Phelps Bultman, AIA, representing the Midlands. Within a few weeks, they obtained the endorsement of the AIA/SC board, and the project was off and running.

The Task Force shaped the book. In the early stages they adopted an outline, established editorial policies, and, working with Hunter Clarkson of Alt Lee, Inc., defined our aspirations for the finished product. Each member gathered research materials, conducted interviews and wrote drafts of sections they found especially interesting. Through statewide mailings and personal calls, they sought materials and support from architects and architectural firms throughout the state. As the book took shape, the Task Force served as an editorial board, reviewing, amending and improving each element of the text. Gayland Witherspoon, FAIA, Executive Director of the Clemson Advancement Foundation for Design + Building, provided important material from the archives at Clemson. Harlan McClure, FAIA and Dean of the College of Architecture, had begun an historical project c. 1981. He had graduate students interview approximately 20 architects across the state, and their tape recordings and an unpublished memoir by McClure – all provided to the Task Force by Witherspoon – preserve memories which otherwise would have been lost.

Hunter Clarkson of Alt Lee, Inc. and his associate Tau Carlisle shaped the piles of pictures and text into a book. Hunter designed the book, selected the paper, dealt with the printer and handled all the minutiae of production. This is the third book we have worked on together. It is always a joy, for where others see pictures, Hunter sees nuances of balance, color intensity, pixels and design potential. Everyone who uses or enjoys the book is indebted to him. Tau Carlisle, made sure things got done on time, and I am especially grateful to him.

At the University of South Carolina, those who were especially helpful included Michael R. Macan and Kate Boyd, reference specialists at Cooper Library, Beth Bilderback, Robin Copp and Thelma M. Hayes of the South Caroliniana Library and Mana Hewitt, computer guru in the Department of Art. Farther afield, Sarah Turner, archivist and records manager at the AIA Knowledge Center, Washington, DC, helped the project along. From the outset we knew that much of our material would be drawn from a collection of cassette tapes, interviews with architects, made in the early 1980s. Carolyn (Mrs. James) Thomas, and administrative staff in various offices transcribed the often difficult-to-understand tapes, and they are the unsung heroes here.

Phelps Bultman prepared a draft focusing on historic preservation and wishes to express his thanks to Rodger Stroup and the staff at the South Carolina Archives and History Center, especially Mary W. Edmonds, Daniel Elswick and Andrew Chandler. Earle Gaulden prepared a draft of the history of the architectural program at Clemson. For the early period of this history, James Thomas, Stephanie Adams and Michael Cole helped gather materials at the Strom Thurmond Institute at Clemson; for the period after 1950, John Jacques, Gayland Witherspoon and Kirk Craig each provided information. James Barker and John M. Mitchell read the Clemson portion of the draft and offered valuable suggestions. Pete McKellar prepared an index of notable articles in the AIA/SC magazine and provided materials relevant to the history of the Board of Architectural Examiners. Working with him, Jan Simpson and Alice Richardson, SC State Board of Architectural Examiners, gathered facts needed to present the history of the board. In addition to chairing our meetings and keeping the project on track, Jim Thomas focused on the section on drawing techniques. Whenever any of us had questions, Tracey B. Waltz, executive director of the chapter, graciously offered information and assistance.

Although they appear up front, "Acknowledgements" are typically written last while memories are fresh. Perhaps my most memorable, happy moments in this project were seeing wonderful, early 20th century drawings in flat files at the Caroliniana Library – Beth Bilderback led me to them – and an urbane, stimulating luncheon, arranged by Theodora Simons, which enabled us to meet the children of Albert Simons and discuss his work prior to World War II.

The working files for the project were housed at the AIA/SC chapter office. Tracey B. Waltz made us feel welcome and provided a pleasant, efficient place to meet and work.

Specific sources are acknowledged in the footnotes and bibliography, but citations don't convey the sense of pleasure and privilege I enjoyed throughout the project. The ideals and aspirations expressed by architects are heartening. Most of them seem happy in their work, and they are good company. Principal sources include interviews with older architects, articles in the AIA/SC magazine, unpublished memoirs and a number of books, including the scarce and wonderful book by Walter Petty, *Architectural Practice in South Carolina, 1913-1963*.

Petty's book has been our main model, but we also often turned to *The South Carolina Architects, 1885-1935, a Biographical Dictionary* by John E. Wells and Robert E. Dalton; these two books are especially useful to anyone interested in the profession in South Carolina.

Finally, on behalf of the History Book Task Force, I want to thank everyone who funded the publication. Individuals and firms who contributed include:

Gold Level
$5000 and above

LS3P Associates Ltd., Charleston

Roger Milliken, Hon. AIA, Spartanburg

South Carolina Chapter of the American Institute of Architects, Columbia

Silver Level
$2500 - $4999

Craig, Gaulden & Davis, Greenville

Lockwood Greene, Spartanburg

The Family of Peter A. McKellar, Mount Pleasant

Stevens & Wilkinson, Columbia

Jim and Carolyn Thomas, Spartanburg

Bronze Level
$1500-$2499

Phelps Bultman, AIA Emeritus, Columbia

Design Partnership, Inc., Greenville

Michael Keeshen, Architect, Greenville

The LPA Group, Inc., Columbia

Marshall Clarke Architects, Inc., Greenville

Neal-Prince & Partners, Greenville

Stubbs Muldrow Herin, Architects, Inc., Mount Pleasant

South Carolina Chapter of the American Society of Landscape Architects

Contributors
$100-$1499

Robert E. Anderson, AIA, Columbia

William H. Anderson, AIA, Columbia

Architects BC, Inc., Lexington

Architrave, Columbia

Ard, Wood, Holcombe & Slate, Inc., Greenville

Architectural Concepts, Inc., Columbia

Paul Brickell, AIA, Greenville

The Boudreaux Group, Inc., Columbia

Catalyst Architects, Columbia

Henry C. Chambers, Hon. AIA, Beaufort

Suzanne Childs, AIA, Greenville

Lynn Craig, AIA, Clemson

Cummings & McCrady, Inc., Charleston

Design Materials, Raleigh

David Eagan, Hon. AIA, Anderson

Enwright Associates, Greenville

Freeman & Major, Architects, PA, Greenville

GMK Associates, Inc., Columbia

Greene & Associates, Architects, Greenville

John Bell Hines, AIA, Spartanburg

Jumper, Carter, Sease Architects, PA, West Columbia

Langley & Associates, Architects, Greer

Lee & Parker, Architects, Hilton Head Island

McCreary/Snow Architects, PA, Columbia

McKellar & Associates, Mount Pleasant

McMillan Smith & Partners, Architects, Spartanburg

Miller/Player & Associates, Greenville

Richard Mitchell, AIA Emeritus, Greenville

H.M. Mooremann, AIA, Aiken

Mozingo-Wallace, Architects, Myrtle Beach

Pazdan-Smith Group, Inc. Architects, Greenville

Rosenblum Coe, Architects, Charleston

Schmitt Sampson Walker Architects, Charleston

Ron Smith, AIA, Spartanburg

Peter Stewart, AIA, Columbia

Stokes Browning, AIA, Greenville

Summers & Associates, Orangeburg

H. Harold Tarleton, FAIA, Greenville

Thomas & Denzinger, Architects, Charleston

Thomas John Gilmore, AIA, Spartanburg

Townsend Architects - Planning Group, Greenville

Tych & Walker, Architects, LLP, Myrtle Beach

Robert Upshur, AIA Emeritus, Columbia

Watson Tate Savory Architects, Inc., Columbia

John W. Weems, Jr., AIA Emeritus, Aiken

Gayland Witherspoon, FAIA, Greenville

Allen Wood, AIA, Florence

Preface

This book recounts the development of the architectural profession in South Carolina and emphasizes the work of the South Carolina Chapter of the American Institute of Architects. Several things prompted the project. There are a number of books about buildings and historic preservation in the state, but there has never been an illustrated overview focusing on the development of architecture as a profession. Other AIA chapters have published books which have proven useful for reference, client development and collegial remembrance. The AIA/SC History Book Task force is keenly aware of the loss of institutional memory as older colleagues leave the stage. This memory is useful, for many of the problems faced by architects reoccur in each generation.

Architects know their designs must facilitate many functions, and this book is like that. The first sections aim to preserve and present the past; the second part focuses on people and firms practicing architecture in South Carolina today. The historical review is based mainly on memoirs by notable architects, for their writings offer an authoritative description of the foundations of the profession. Awards and honors given by the American Institute of Architects and its components create an informal portrait of the profession today. Celebrating design award winners and those who have made notable civic and professional contributions allows us to show how architects enhance the built environment and reinforce the sense of place which makes us all feel at home.

Most families have boxes of pictures and papers they intend to organize some day. The urge to pass along knowledge is a deeply human trait, and we try to do that in the pictures and text that follow.

Not surprisingly, the growth of the state over the last half-century has been paralleled by the growth of the architectural profession. Membership in the AIA/SC has grown from six charter members in June 1913, to 790 (out of 973 licensed architects residing in South Carolina and 2251 out-of-state registrants) in June 2001. Seventeen architects now practicing in South Carolina are nationally recognized as Fellows of the American Institute of Architects, and a South Carolinian, Thompson Penney, FAIA, will serve as president of the AIA in 2003. It is a good time to pause and survey the state of the profession in South Carolina.

THE AMERICAN INSTITUTE OF ARCHITECTS

Thompson E. Penney, FAIA
2002 First Vice President/President Elect

    I can remember vividly being called to the front of the room during the annual business meeting of AIA South Carolina in 1976. I was presented with a copy of *Architectural Practice in South Carolina, 1913-1963*. This gift represented my passage of the architectural examination and induction into corporate membership in AIA South Carolina. It was a meaningful and symbolic gift, inextricably linking professional passage with professional opportunities.

    I am thrilled that *Architectural Practice: The South Carolina Chapter of the American Institute of Architects* will carry on the linkage between the AIA and architectural practice in South Carolina. It traces our roots as a profession in South Carolina, and the voices of the past echo throughout its pages. Many of the early drawings and memoirs, never published before, are inspirational, and new facts and historical insights abound. Anyone interested in South Carolina architecture will find this volume useful as an orientation, as an aid to memory and as a reference. You can flip through it, dip into it, or read and savor it.

    Everyone involved is to be commended. The donors listed in the acknowledgements made it possible, and the AIA/SC History Book Task Force - Phelps Bultman, AIA, Earle Gaulden, FAIA, Pete McKellar, AIA and James Thomas, FAIA, Chairman - designer, Hunter Clarkson of Alt Lee, Inc., and author, Professor John M. Bryan, Hon. AIA, have worked together for more than a year to produce it.

    The vitality of a professional organization depends on the interest members take in their common values, goals and culture, coupled with the effectiveness of their public outreach. By presenting a selection of notable buildings in an accessible, attractive and permanent way, this book will further the goals of AIA South Carolina and its local components.

    Albert Simons, FAIA, who helped initiate the preservation movement in Charleston, Bryan writes "held the past and present in an harmonious balance." This book does just that.

    We are all stewards of the future. I can think of no better way to prepare for the future than to study the past.

Thompson E. Penney, FAIA
2003 President
The American Institute of Architects

LS3P ASSOCIATES LTD.
24 North Market Street, Suite 300
Charleston, SC 29401
Telephone 843.577.4444
Facsimile 843.722.4789
Email: penney@ls3p.com

Chapter One
History, c. 1735-1955

Architecture is the most social of the plastic arts. Painting, sculpture and the crafts are typically created by people working alone, but architecture, on the other hand, is inherently collaborative. The history of architectural practice in South Carolina is a story of increasing collaboration, cooperation and interaction. Major milestones in this story include the early untrained practitioners (c. 1735-1820) who gave way to architects with specific training in the early 19th century, then shortly after the Civil War, architectural firms emerged and began to dominate the field. Early in the 20th century, the seeds of an architectural curriculum were planted in the Department of Engineering at Clemson College, then the American Institute of Architects South Carolina Chapter was founded (1913), and a professional license was required by law (1917). Each stage of the profession's development reflects a trend toward increasingly complex relationships between the architect, the architectural profession, and society at large.

The Earliest Architects in South Carolina, c. 1735-1820

Charles Chassereau was among the first – and possibly was the very first – to present himself to the public as an architect in South Carolina. In January 1735, he advertised in the South Carolina Gazette that he had recently come from London and would "draw Plans and Elevations of all kinds of Buildings, both civil and Military, like wise perspective Views of prospects of Towns or Gentlemen's Houses or Plantations, he calculates Estimates for Buildings or Repairs, inspects and measures Artificer's Works, [and] sets out grounds for Gardens or Parks."[1]

Throughout the 1700s, all along the eastern seaboard, architecture was in the hands of three distinct groups. First, immigrants, like Chassereau, advertised design services, usually stressing their familiarity with European styles; secondly, in the major seaports there were also carpenters and builders hoping to better themselves by designing as well as building; and finally, there were gentlemen amateurs whose social prominence, libraries and travels enabled them to design for and influence friends and relatives. All three groups relied heavily on

---

[1] Mills Lane, *Architecture of the Old South, South Carolina* (Savannah: Beehive Press, 1997), 33; Anna Wells Rutledge, *Artists in the Life of Charleston* (Columbia: University of South Carolina Press, 1980), 113.

illustrations in English and European architectural books. Throughout the Georgian (c. 1730-1775) and Federal periods (c. 1775-1810), architectural design in North America was typically done "by the book."

In Charleston, Saint Michael's (1752-1761) and the Exchange (1766) provide apt examples of the influence of pattern books on immigrant designers and local builders. St. Michael's was said to be "built on the plan of one of Mr. Gibson's designs" – probably a garbled reference to James Gibbs' *Book of Architecture* which contained detailed engravings – plans, sections and elevations – of James Gibbs' design for St. Martin's in the Fields, erected in London in 1726. Samuel Cardy, the Charleston contractor who built St. Michael's, used Gibbs' plate 29 for the steeple and simplified Gibbs' illustrations of St. Martin's nave and portico.

Alternate Steeple Designs
for St. Martin's in the Fields, London
James Gibbs, *Book of Architecture*, 1728

Photograph by the author

St. Michael's Church, Charleston, SC

Market Hall, Chipping Camden, England

Market Hall, Wyndham, England

Winnsboro Town Clock

The Exchange in Charleston was designed by William Rigby Naylor using the English town and market hall tradition of an open, pedestrian-oriented arcade at grade and enclosed office and meeting space above. Naylor probably referred to pattern books, but even if he did not, his basic idea for the Exchange was drawn from the ancient building type, examples of which, dating from the 16th through the 19th centuries, still stand throughout England. From Charleston this building type spread across South Carolina – the Rice Mill in Georgetown, the Town Hall in Cheraw, the first City Hall in Columbia, the Town Clock in Winnsboro, and finally, coming full circle, Edward Brickell White's Market in Charleston.

Despite occasional major commissions, none of the colonial American seaports offered enough business to justify the establishment of purely architectural offices. Practitioners, like Chassereau, who advertised architectural services, typically also offered a cafeteria-like array of lessons in geometry, drawing, surveying, and other skills. For example, in Charleston a stonecutter from Edinburgh, Thomas Walker, who sold tombstones, also "opened an evening school for teaching the rules of Architecture, from seven to nine in the evening (four nights a week)." Another advertisement tells us that M. Depresseville "continues to keep his Drawing School, in different Part of Landscapes, with Pencil or Washed, teaches Architecture, and to draw with method; also the necessary acknowledgements for the Plans." Also in Charleston, Blakeleay White advertised instruction in the "principles of Modern Architecture, with drawing and designing, not only theoretically but practically." White's lessons included building a model house.

Robert Mills (1781-1855) – the future architect – was an adolescent in Charleston in 1795, when his older brother Thomas advertised lessons in every "branch of useful and polite literature," French, Latin and Greek, geometry, trigonometry, and "the principles of modern architecture, with drawing and designing." In describing the architectural portion of the curriculum, Thomas Mills' advertisement said "at the commencement of this very useful undertaking the complete frame of a double three story house, in miniature, will be raised, and lectures given explanatory of the subject by way of exhibiting to the friends of the young gentlemen a specimen of the manner in which this business will be conducted; by this method it will be evident, that a person may soon become a complete architect or master builder."[2]

---

[2] John M. Bryan, *America's First Architect, Robert Mills* (New York: Princeton Architectural Press, 2001), 8. In addition to my recent book, there are two earlier biographies of Mills: Rhodri W. Liscombe, *Altogether American* (New York: Oxford University Press, 1994) and Helen Pierce Mar Gallagher, *Robert Mills, Architect of the Washington Monument* (New York: Columbia University Press, 1935). All three contain citations and bibliographies.

The Exchange and Custom House, Charleston, SC

Exchange and Customs House, Charleston, SC
William Rigby Naylor, architect.
Courtesy of the South Carolina Archives and History Center.

The work of Gabriel Manigault (1758-1809) exemplifies the impact of the gentleman amateur in early South Carolina. His designs embody his mastery of the precise and delicate English Adam Style, and the jewel-like, diminutive gate house (c. 1802-1803) which he designed for his brother, Joseph Manigault, suggests that like Naylor and Cardy, Gabriel Manigault drew inspiration from the pattern books.

Robert Mills' First Competition and the State of the Profession, 1802

If advertisements record the beginnings of the profession in South Carolina, the 1802 competition for the South Carolina College is a notable benchmark. The contest was advertised nationally, and the diverse backgrounds of the contestants (including a scientist, college presidents, a builder and an amateur) reflect the state of the profession. Robert Mills, then a student, won half the prize (the first design for which he was paid), and the best trained architect in the country, Benjamin Henry Latrobe, wrote the college trustees a scathing critique of competitions in which he described problems that continued to plague architects into the 20th century.

In addition to Mills, the contestants included Asa Messer, the third president of Brown University; S. Stanhope Smith, who was the president of the College of New Jersey in Princeton; Peter Banner, a carpenter builder then erecting buildings at Yale which had been designed by the painter, John Trumbull; Benjamin Silliman, a scientist at Yale, and Hugh Smith, an amateur from Charleston. Latrobe was the only professional architect who responded to the South Carolina College competition. The trustees apparently wrote him, and he sent a "fair sketch" accompanied by a long letter pointing out that he disapproved of competitions because he found it "inconvenient and humiliating" to prepare drawings which would be judged by non-professionals merely "for the chance of being preferred to the amateur, and workmen who may enter the lists against me." Latrobe said competition winners were usually people "possessing the confidence of building committees, or holding a seat in the committee" and the situation "often made me repent that I have cultivated my profession in preference to my farm."[3]

The trustees' decision proved Latrobe right. They split the $300 prize between Mills and Smith – two neophytes and the only native South Carolinians who entered the competition. The trustees then drew their own plan resembling Nassau Hall at Princeton where most of them had been students.

---

3 Ibid., 123-125. For a full account of the South Carolina College competition see the author's *An Architectural History of the South Carolina College* (Columbia: University of South Carolina Press, 1976).

Mills' two surviving drawings for the South Carolina College competition had no influence on the buildings (Rutledge and Dessassure Colleges) which were erected, but the drawings show his ability as a draftsman and designer as he entered Latrobe's office in 1803, and they provide a glimpse of what architectural drawings were like as the profession was getting underway in America. Pen and ink and watercolor wash on paper, the drawings show Federal Style motifs on the facades – Palladian windows, fanlights, round-headed windows and the cupola – awkwardly juxtaposed with projecting Regency features – the central and end bays, stair tower and parapets. The surviving ground plan ignores some of the criteria required by the trustees, for plans were supposed to provide student and faculty residences and classrooms, yet Mills made no provision for closets, water closets or rooms *en suite*.

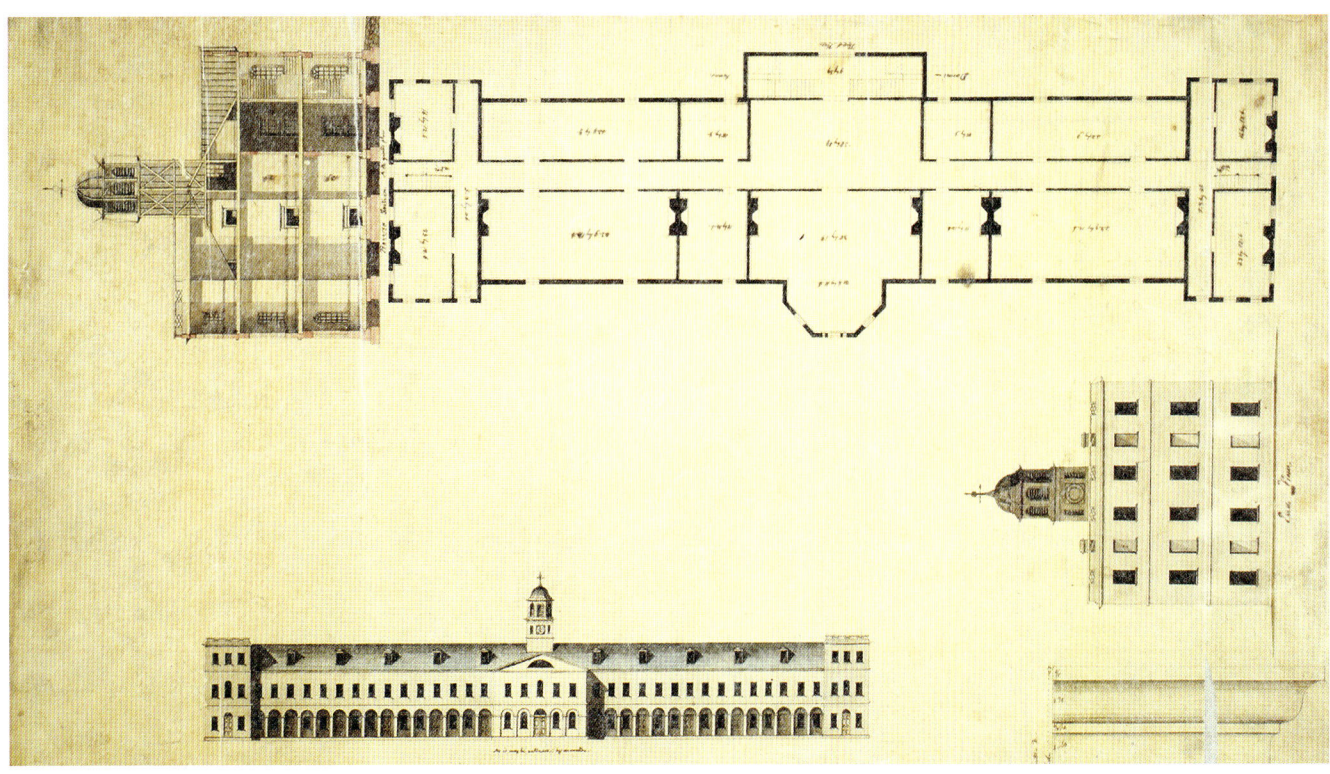

Proposal for the South Carolina College
Robert Mills, architect
Courtesy of the South Carolina Archives and History Center

The most notable aspect of Mills' design was an open arcade at the base of the rear façade to provide covered access to the ground floor classrooms. Nothing like this existed in America at the time. This concept has become ubiquitous in suburban schools, but Mills proposed it a decade before Jefferson first used it at the University of Virginia.

There are several possible sources for Mills' proposed arcade. He knew the town and market hall building type, and through prints he no doubt also knew the arcaded academic quadrangles of Oxford and Cambridge. He may have discussed the South Carolina competition with Jefferson and adapted the president's earlier (1771-1772) proposal for an addition to the College of William and Mary – an arcaded quadrangle.[4] The Revolution thwarted the William and Mary project, but the reappearance of colonnades at the University of Virginia some forty years later suggests Jefferson never lost sight of their usefulness in an academic setting.

The Antebellum Years, c. 1820-1860

Photograph by Robert M. Smith, Jr.

Maxcy Monument
Robert Mills, architect

The antebellum years, c. 1820-1860, saw a shift toward reliance on professional architects for major projects. The declining influence of gentleman amateurs and carpenter builders was quite dramatic. An apt turning point, like the pin of a hinge, was the million-dollar appropriation by the State of South Carolina in 1820. This money was to be spent on the statewide development of courthouses, jails, bridges and canals. Robert Mills and Abram Blanding were retained to direct these projects. Mills worked primarily as an architect, designing 17 courthouses, 13 jails, an insane asylum, a fireproof records office and a gunpowder magazine complex. Blanding worked as a civil engineer, concentrating on canals and bridges. Mills' work for the internal improvements program required sophisticated design and embodied his concern for fireproof construction throughout the state.

---

[4] William Howard Adams, ed., *The Eye of Thomas Jefferson* (Charlottesville: Thomas Jefferson Memorial Foundation, 1976), figure 23, page 19.

"Mr. Jefferson's Lawn," the Library and Colonnades at the University of Virginia
Thomas Jefferson, architect

Details of the Colonnades at the University of Virginia
Thomas Jefferson, architect.

The Legacy of Robert Mills

Many Carolinians have made notable contributions to our national culture and history, but none has played a more formative role – in any field of endeavor – than Mills did in American architecture. He was the first native-born American to train specifically for a career as an architect. During the 1830s and 1840s, as the most active architect in Washington, DC, he helped define the architectural presence of the federal government. He designed the U.S. Treasury, the General Post Office, the Washington National Monument and portions of the Patent Office. He established design criteria for the Smithsonian and directed the initial construction of the building designed by James Renwick. Mills was among the first to propose enlarging the U.S. Capitol by adding wings and elevating the dome (a similar plan by Thomas U. Walter of Philadelphia was adopted despite Mills' objections and appeals).

Eliza Barnwell Smith Mills and Robert Mills , c. 1850
From the author's collection

Beyond architecture, Mills published books and pamphlets on navigation, transportation, cartography and engineering. His *American Pharos or Lighthouse Guide* is among the earliest comprehensive guides to American beacons, buoys and lights; his *Atlas of South Carolina* presented the first systematic mapping of any state; his "Plan of a Railroad" proposed an elevated monorail and his manuscript "Rotary Steam Engine" presented plans for a fuel efficient, vibration free rotary piston engine.

Mills' federal work, done in the 1830s and 1840s, is rooted in the modular, fireproof masonry groin vaults he practiced and perfected in South Carolina during the 1820s. He made fireproof construction a federal standard, and because his mature, federal work happily coincided with the Jacksonian budget surplus, he was able to plan and build on a scale without precedent in America, a grand, monumental scale which matched his vision of our destiny.

Despite Mills' courthouses across the state, during this period, cultural life remained centered in Charleston, and although the city's population grew slowly (from 37,471 in 1820 to 40,195 in 1860), wealth and a sense of civic destiny prompted the construction of numerous public and institutional buildings, and this drew architects. Local carpenter-builders – like Frederick Wesner (1788-1848) who designed St. John's Lutheran Church (1815) and the Old Citadel (c 1830) – began to face competition from newcomers like Russell Warren (1783-1860) from Rhode Island who advertised himself as a "house wright," or the enigmatic Joseph Hyde (n.d.) who was active in Charleston c. 1835-1838 and apparently designed the second St. Philip's Church (1836).

Photograph by the author

The South Carolina Asylum
Robert Mills, architect

Photograph by the author

The South Carolina Asylum
Robert Mills, architect

The South Carolina Asylum
Robert Mills, architect
Courtesy of the South Carolina Archives and History Center

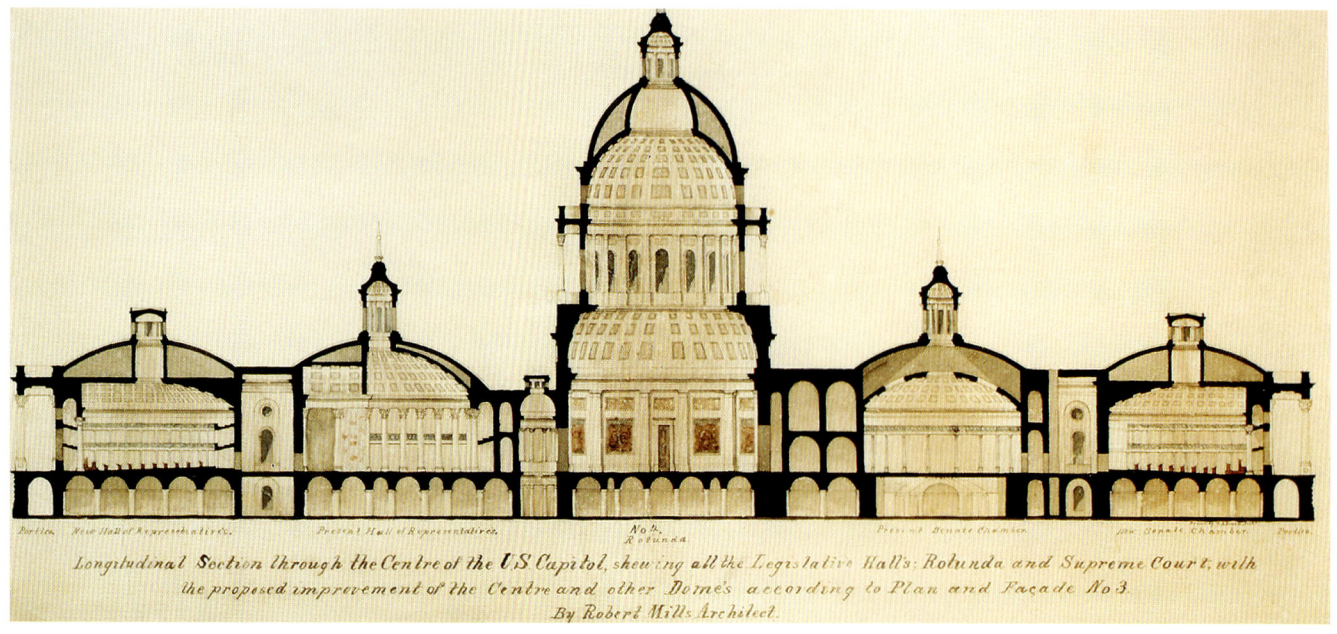

Proposed Expansion of the U.S. Capitol
Robert Mills, architect
Courtesy of the Office of the Architect of the U.S. Capitol

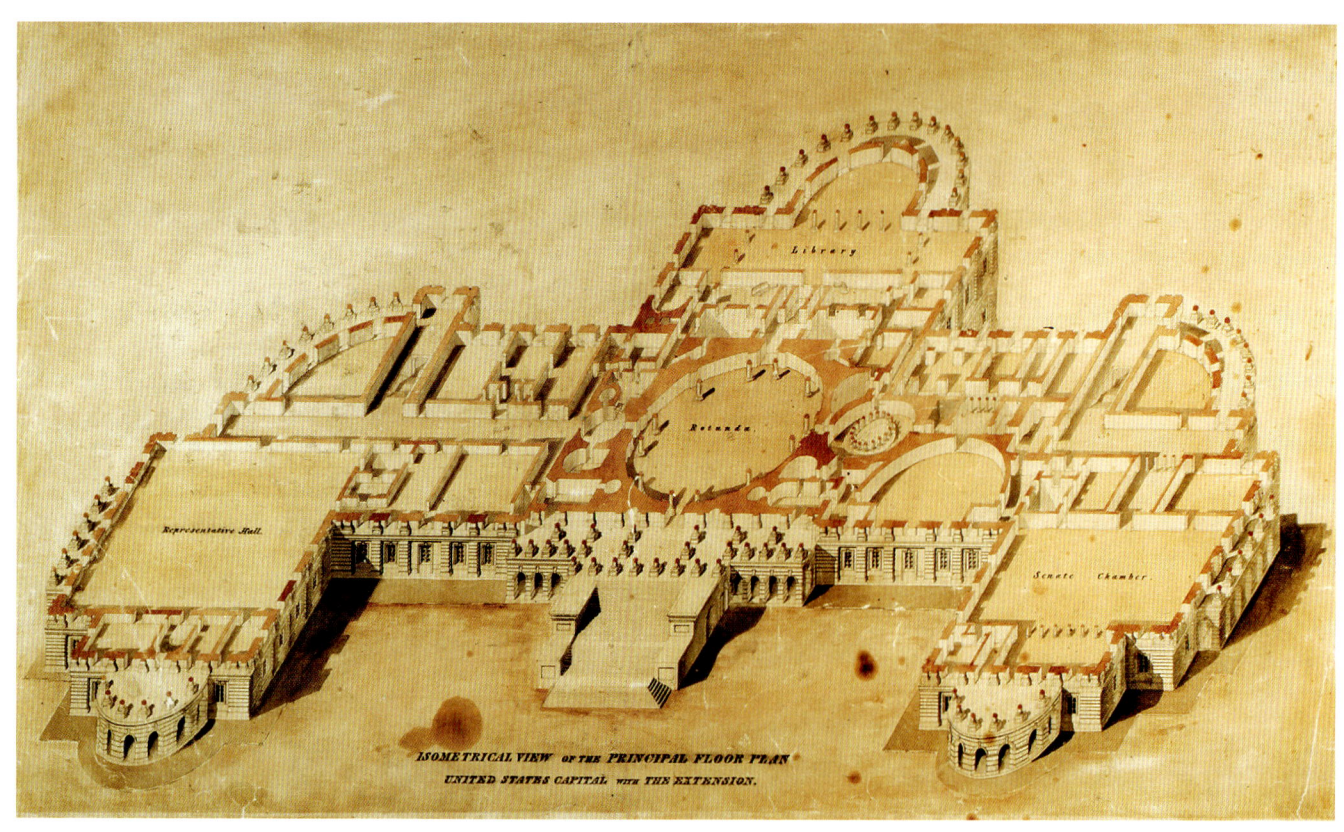

Proposed Expansion of the U.S. Capitol
Robert Mills, architect
Courtesy of the Office of the Architect of the U.S. Capitol

Proposal for the Washington National Monument
Robert Mills, architect
Courtesy of the National Archives of the United States

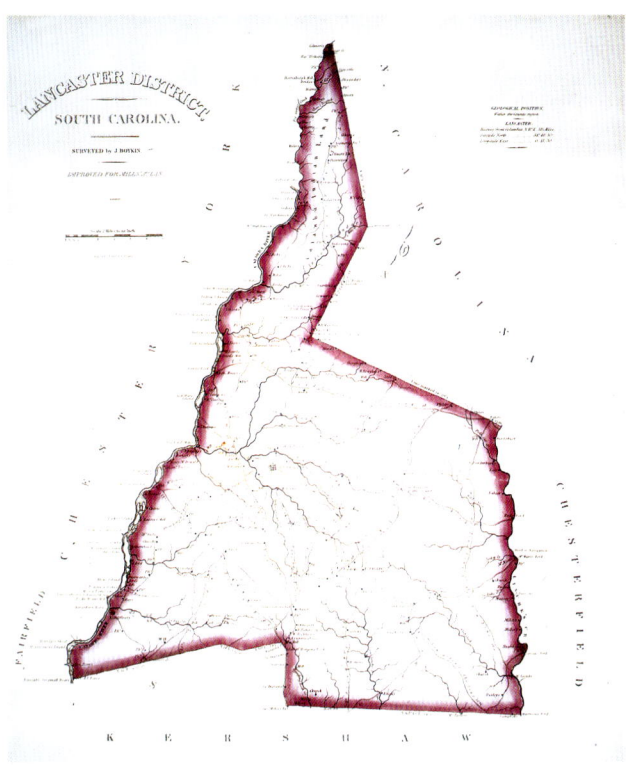

Lancaster District from the *Atlas of South Carolina*
Robert Mills, architect and engineer
Courtesy of the South Caroliniana Library

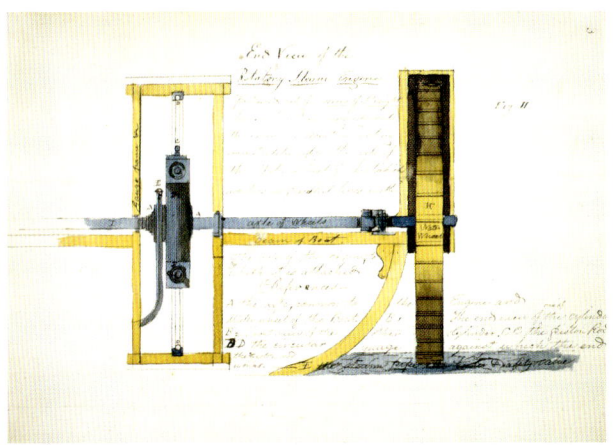

Proposal for a Rotary Piston Engine
Robert Mills, architect and engineer
Courtesy of the Franklin Institute

Proposal for a Rotary Piston Engine
Robert Mills, architect and engineer
Courtesy of the Franklin Institute

Now major commissions often went to outsiders such as William Strickland (1787-1854) who had trained briefly with Mills in Latrobe's office and whose practice was based in Philadelphia (Strickland designed the first major building at the College of Charleston), or Thomas Ustick Walter (1804-1887), a protégé of Strickland's. Walter designed the Hibernian Society Hall (1839-1840). Charles F. Reichardt, from Germany and New York, designed the Charleston Hotel (1839), a grandstand for the Washington Racetrack, a steeple for Mills' Circular Church and other public works (none of his work survives). In 1839, when Governor John L. Manning decided to build Milford in Stateburg – the finest Greek Revival residence in the state – he called on Nathaniel F. Potter (1807-1874) of Providence, Rhode Island.

Milford was still new when Gov. Manning initiated construction (1851) on a new state capitol in Columbia. Peter H. Hammarsköld, who had immigrated from Sweden, was selected as architect. He designed a masonry vaulted, fireproof raised basement adjacent the first State House in Columbia. Hammarsköld's wing was intended to serve as the ground floor of a wholly new State House, but just as it was nearing completion, the foundation settled; the arches spread, and the vaulting collapsed. Hammarsköld's successor, George Edward Walker of Charleston, was quickly replaced by John Rudolph Niernsee, an architect and engineer whose office was located in Baltimore. Niernsee designed the present State House (1854) and moved to Columbia and directed construction until work was halted in 1861 by the Civil War.[5]

A handful of native South Carolinians – all of whom were based in Charleston – established themselves as worthy competitors of the outsiders during the antebellum years. Edward Brickell White (1806-1882) was adept in several styles. His memorable buildings include the gate lodge at the College of Charleston, and the Charleston Market Hall, both being Classical Revival. White also designed a series of Gothic Revival churches – Trinity in Abbeville, Trinity in Columbia and the French Huguenot Church in Charleston – and the Georgian steeple of St. Philip's in Charleston. Edward C. Jones (active c. 1848-1861) and Francis D. Lee (1826-1885), who worked together as Jones and Lee, Architects from 1852 until 1857, were eclectic, superb stylists. They were the premier architectural firm based in South Carolina during the antebellum years. They designed Number One Broad Street (1853), the Renaissance Revival commercial building that anchors a corner opposite Naylor's Exchange,

---

[5] For a sweeping analysis of antebellum architecture in Charleston, see Kenneth Severens, *Charleston, Antebellum Architecture and Civic Destiny* (Knoxville: University of Tennessee Press, 1988); for concise information on the careers of individual architects, see Beatrice St. Julian Ravenel, *Architects of Charleston* (Charleston: Carolina Art Association, 1964).

Porter's Lodge, College of Charleston
Edward Brickell White, architect
Courtesy of the Library of Congress

Charleston Hotel, 1865
Courtesy of the Library of Congress

Milford Plantation
Historic American Buildings Survey
Courtesy of the Library of Congress

Detail of Milford Plantation, Historic American Buildings Survey, Courtesy of the Library of Congress

and Lee is also responsible for the Moorish style Farmer's and Exchange Bank (1853-1854) at 141 East Bay, an exotic façade of Connecticut brownstone.

Re-Building: The New South after Reconstruction, c. 1880-1913

The Civil War stymied the development of the architectural profession in South Carolina for 30 years. Lacking work, many architects moved away. John Rudolph Niernsee, for example, returned to Baltimore; Edward C. Jones moved to Memphis in 1867; Francis D. Lee went to St. Louis in 1868, and Edward Brickell White re-established himself in New York in 1879. When the economy slowly began to recover in the 1880s, the tide turned and several enduring changes quickly became evident. First, major projects were no longer concentrated in Charleston (as had been the case prior to the Civil War). And secondly, new building types – textile mills and mill villages, skyscrapers and public schools and hospitals – signified important cultural changes across the Piedmont and Upcountry. As a direct consequence of industrial, commercial and public spending, architects and architectural firms appeared across the state, like mushrooms after summer rain.

In the 1880s and 1890s, architectural offices, which often specialized in one or more of the new building types, opened in Florence, Columbia, Anderson, Greenville and Spartanburg. Out-of-state architects were again attracted to South Carolina to compete for the new work. The competition for the completion of the State House in 1888 provides a glimpse of the profession as the 19th century drew to a close.

The state commissioners in charge of the competition advertised in the *Columbia Daily Register* and the *Charleston News and Courier*. They probably assumed that a residency requirement, low salary and the political climate all meant they must search for a native South Carolinian. Despite limited circulation, the notice produced "a voluminous batch of papers" from at least 13 applicants. Nine applications came from South Carolinians (four from Columbia, three from Charleston and two from Greenville); the others came from North Carolina, Alabama, Arkansas and Washington, DC. The applicants are rarely remembered today: "F. Niernsee, Columbia, H. Gabler, Greenville, Tilman Watson, Columbia, Geo. W. Waring, Columbia, E.B. Rutledge, Greenville, T.J. Schmidt, Columbia, Mess, Abrams and Seylr[?], Charleston, L.R. Gibbes, Charleston, E.R.[J.] White, Charleston, A.J. Armstrong, Birmingham, Ala., B.J.Barlett, Little Rock, Arkansas, Byron A. Purgin, Greensboro, NC. and J.F. Denson, Washington, DC."[6]

---

[6] John M. Bryan, *Creating the South Carolina State House* (Columbia: University of South Carolina Press, 1999), 102.

Photograph by Alt Lee, Inc.

North Facade of State House with Confederate Monument.

Although they submitted their applications separately, E.J. White of Charleston and Francis (Frank) McHenry Niernsee, joined forces and were hired as White and Niernsee, Architects, at a salary of $1,800 each per year. Frank Niernsee's father, John Rudolph Niernsee of Baltimore, had designed the State House, but he died before work resumed after the Civil War. White played no role as an architect at the State House, for White and Niernsee was dissolved on October 1, 1888, and Frank Niernsee was then appointed "sole Architect at a salary of $2,100 per annum."

Frank Niernsee was energetic and gregarious, and like his father, he felt at home in South Carolina. He kept a twisted artillery fragment on his desk, and when visitors picked it up he would recount the morning of February 17, 1865, when the shell struck the State House while he was crossing the grounds as a Confederate cavalry courier. He had been born in Baltimore in 1849 and was five years old when the family first moved south. Throughout his childhood and adolescence his father was working on the State House. When the war broke out Frank and his older brother volunteered. Both survived unscathed, and when the family returned north after the war, Frank studied engineering at the University of Virginia and then joined his father's office in Baltimore in 1878.

We do not know exactly when Frank Niernsee returned to South Carolina. As early as 1875 he presented material on the construction of roads to the Reconstruction legislature (nothing came of this). He may have accompanied his father on a visit in 1882 and decided to stay, for Frank Niernsee's obituary says he moved back in 1882. John R. Niernsee moved back to Columbia in 1885, but none of the records indicate that Frank came with him. In 1887 the local newspaper noted that drawings and specifications for the restoration of the Colleton County courthouse and jail in Walterboro could be seen in Frank Niernsee's office, and this is the earliest evidence that he was in business in Columbia. In 1888 he was listed as an architect for the first time in the city directories as "White and Niernsee, State House"[7]

Unlike his father, Frank Niernsee did not focus exclusively on the State House, for the job was no longer considered full-time and did not pay a living wage. In addition to working at the State House, he designed St. Paul's Lutheran Church and Chapel in Columbia (1888), prepared plans for St. Peter's Catholic Church, Columbia (1889), was hired to construct a cotton seed oil mill in Winnsboro (1889) and designed

---

[7] Bryan, *Creating the South Carolina State House*, 103.

municipal water works (1891-1894) for Columbia. In nearby Sumter he designed a school and jail and sheriff's residence (1891-1892). In 1893 he formed a partnership with A.G. LaMotte, the young engineer who examined the State House after the earthquake, and as Niernsee and LaMotte they were responsible for at least 15 architectural and engineering projects in the Midlands before their association ended in 1896. Together they designed individual residential and institutional buildings, but they also published an updated map of Columbia (1895) and designed the mill village of New Brookland for the Columbia Mills Company (1896).

Frank Niernsee appears to be the earliest architect based in Columbia with a recognizably modern office. Others had advertised as architects prior to 1882, but none of them retained draftsmen or simultaneously serviced a variety of clients in various locations. Frank Niernsee, on the other hand, maintained two offices, one in the State House and a private office at 1528 Main Street, and both offices were busy enough to justify salaried assistants. At the State House, Edwin J. White was the assistant until White and Niernsee was dissolved on October 1, 1888, and White was replaced by Charles Schramm. That spring George Waring joined the State House office as supervising architect "under the direction of the architect," for the commissioners concluded that Frank Niernsee's private business had grown and was taking him away from the State House. Gadsden E. Shand, having just graduated from the South Carolina College, replaced Charles Schramm as draftsman in the State House office in June 1889, and Shand moved to Niernsee's private office the following month and worked there until September 1890. Shand then left to study engineering at the School of Mines at Columbia University in New York. A.G. LaMotte took Shand's place in the private office and worked with Niernsee until 1896. Niernsee needed assistants, for reconstruction, literally, had begun in the South.

Niernsee's staff reflected a growing class of urban professionals whose livelihoods did not depend upon antebellum agrarian skills. In this regard, the career of Gadsden E. Shand is especially telling. After studying in New York, Shand returned to Columbia and became chief engineer of W.B. Smith Whaley and Company. (Shand's early career is important in the evolution of the State House, for at the turn of the century he would be among the first to propose a dome in lieu of John R. Niernsee's tower.)[8]

---

[8] For more on Gadsden E. Shand, see: Bryan, *Creating the South Carolina State House*, 104-105, 113-116.

The Textile Industry
A New Scale of Design and Construction in South Carolina

The Whaley Company specialized in the design of textile mills and designed or expanded 20 mills – fifteen in South Carolina and others in Alabama, Georgia, North Carolina and Massachusetts. In Columbia Whaley designed and had an interest in the Richland Cotton Mill (now called the Whaley Mill) (1895), Granby Cotton Mills (1897), Olympia Cotton Mills (1899) and the Capital City Mills (1900). Although technologically advanced, Whaley's own mills were under capitalized, and at the turn of the century a combination of labor problems, fluctuating prices and accumulated debt forced him into bankruptcy.

Whaley left South Carolina in 1903, but Shand stayed, and for twenty years he focused on the practice of architecture. Initially, he worked alone, and the major surviving work from his early practice is the Richardsonian Romanesque Canal Dime Savings Bank (1893) on Main Street in Columbia. From 1903 through 1912 he worked in partnership with George E. Lafaye as Shand and Lafaye, Architects and Engineers. Together they designed the five-story, reinforced concrete Ottaray Hotel (1907-1908) in Greenville, and numerous banks, schools and commercial buildings throughout South Carolina, North Carolina and Georgia. Their major surviving buildings in Columbia include the Shandon Baptist Church (1908) (now the Bethel A.M.E. Church), the Waverly School (1910), the YMCA building (1911), the Elmwood Baptist Church (1911) and the Columbia City Jail (1912). Shand left architecture in 1912 to form Shand Engineering Company and for two more decades specialized in "industrial power, water power projects, and municipal works."[9]

W.B. Smith Whaley and Co. maintained an architectural department which designed commercial, religious, institutional and residential buildings as well as the mills for which they are remembered. With their peers noted below, they created or transformed many communities across the Piedmont and Upcountry. Architecturally speaking, the impact was dramatic, for the old timber-framed mills driven by water wheels – typically run by a family and perhaps a few paid hands - were replaced by multi-story mills containing machinery for each stage of the spinning and weaving process. The new mills were typically powered by their own generating plants and flanked by housing and community buildings for hundreds of operatives.[10]

---

[9] Bryan, *Creating the South Carolina State House*, 105.

[10] W.B. Smith Whaley and Company, *Modern Cotton Mill Engineering* (Columbia: The State, 1903). I am grateful to Phelps Bultman for bringing this book to my attention.

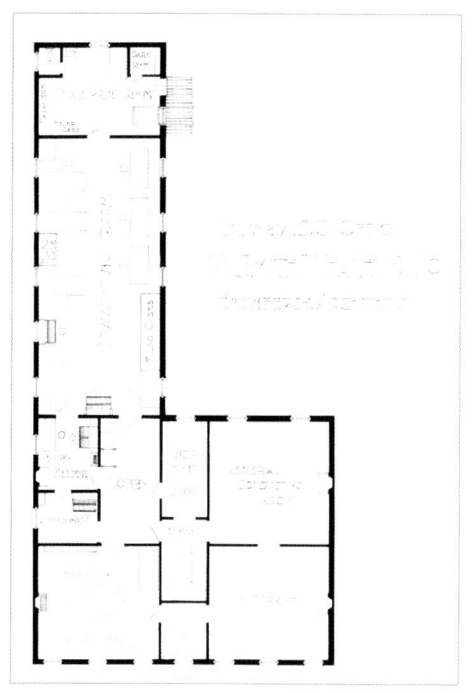

Columbia, SC Office, W.B. Smith Whaley & Co., Engineers & Architects
Reproduced from W.B. Smith Whaley & Co., *Modern Cotton Mill Engineering* (1903)

Photo by W.B. Smith Whaley & Co.
Old Over-shot Wheel
Within Stone's Throw of the Olympia Power Plant
Reproduced from W.B. Smith Whaley & Co., *Modern Cotton Mill Engineering* (1903)

Seneca Cotton Mills, Seneca, SC, W.B. Smith Whaley & Co.
Reproduced from W.B. Smith Whaley & Co., *Modern Cotton Mill Engineering* (1903)

It is worth noting that the textile engineering firms introduced the full service, multi-faceted design team – one office offering architectural design as well as structural and mechanical engineering services. As a designer, the modern architect may be a descendant of Robert Mills, but the typical, modern architectural office owes a great deal to the orchestration of specialties that came to South Carolina with the textile engineers. Equally notable, the mills introduced a new architectural scale to the state. The Seneca Cotton Mill, for example, designed by Whaley and typical of the type, was 77 feet wide, 220 feet long with 19 bays, each being four stories tall and each story being 15 feet high. The central tower (and this too was typical) contained staircases and a water tank for the sprinkler system.

In the Piedmont, the architectural and engineering firms founded by Amos D. Lockwood (1811-1874) and Joseph E. Sirrine (1872-1947) embody almost every aspect of the changes that were reshaping the state and the architectural profession as the 19th century came to a close. Shortly before the Civil War, Lockwood had begun work as a mill engineer in Maine. In 1882 he and Stephen Greene established Lockwood, Greene and Co. in Providence, Rhode Island, a center of New England's textile industry. Designing mills and related buildings, they moved south with the textile industry and opened a branch office in Greenville, South Carolina in 1898. By the time they established their base in Greenville, they already had designed 33 mills in the state, including facilities in Graniteville, Lancaster, Charleston, Pelzer, Pacolet, Darlington, Whitney, Spartanburg, Camden, Lockhart, Newberry, Greenwood and Abbeville. Between 1873 and 1952, Lockwood himself, and later Lockwood, Greene and Co., was responsible for 117 South Carolina projects, and these commissions often entailed multiple buildings. For example: 22 residences for the Langley Cotton Mills (1923); 55 operatives' houses for the Joanna Mills in Goldville (1925); 45 residences for the Pacific Mills in Lyman (1927); 70 more residences in Goldville (1928); and 49 residences for Kendall Mills, Edgefield (1929).[11]

Lockwood, Greene and Co. should be credited with establishing the New England textile mills as a building type in South Carolina. Historically, their most notable single building may be the Columbia Duck Mill which opened in 1894 and was the first textile mill in the world designed to be operated wholly by electric power.[12]

---

[11] John E. Wells and Robert E. Dalton, *The South Carolina Architects, 1885-1935, A Biographical Directory* (Richmond: New South Architectural Press, 1992), 107-112. Also see: William J. Heiser, *Lockwood Greene, 1958-1968, Another Period in the History of an Engineering Business* (Lockwood Greene Engineers, Inc., 1970).

[12] John M. Bryan, *The South Carolina State Museum* (Columbia: SC Museum Foundation, 2000), 14-15.

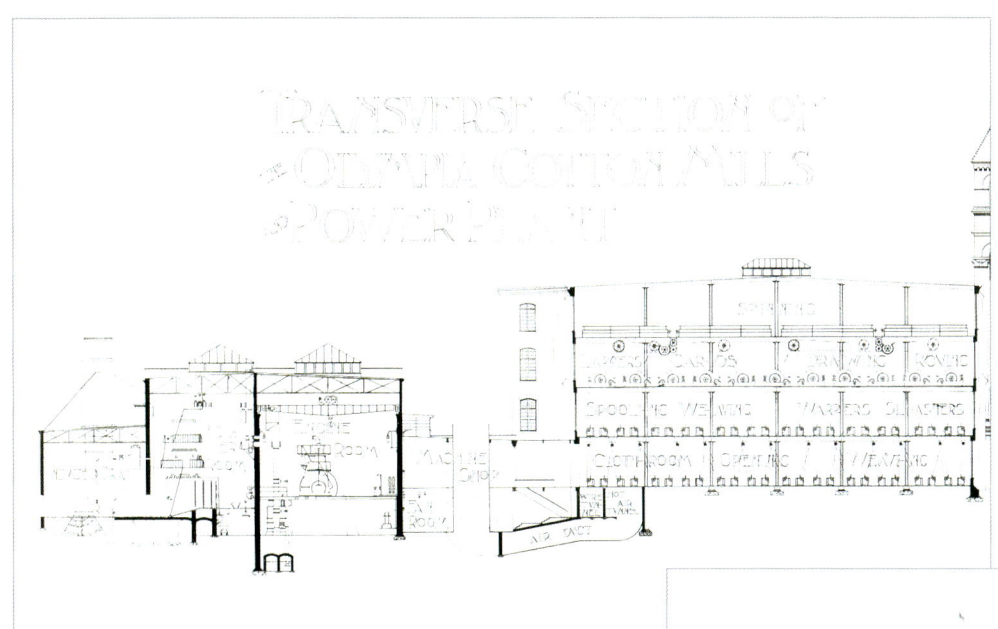

Transverse Section of Olympia Cotton Mills & Power Plant, W.B. Smith Whaley & Co. Reproduced from W.B. Smith Whaley & Co., *Modern Cotton Mill Engineering* (1903)

The Olympia Cotton Mill, W.B. Smith Whaley & Co. Reproduced from W.B. Smith Whaley & Co., *Modern Cotton Mill Engineering* (1903)

Columbia Duck Mill and new electric power station, Lockwood, Greene and Company, c. 1905

Joseph Emory Sirrine first worked for Lockwood, Greene and Co. as a surveyor for the F.W. Poe Mill in Greenville in 1895. When Lockwood, Greene and Co. opened the office in Greenville, Sirrine became its first manager. He left Lockwood, Greene and Co. to establish his own company in 1903. Reorganized as J.E. Sirrine and Co., Engineers, in 1921, Sirrine became "the most important industrial architect and engineer to practice in South Carolina. The emerging industrial complexes of South Carolina's Appalachian corridor, including mills, warehouses, worker housing, schools, commercial buildings, and related structures, owed their form and structure more to Sirrine than to any other architect. Sirrine's work spanned five decades and included projects as far away as Texas and Maine."[13] He was active as an industrialist serving as a vice president of 4 textile companies and a director of 19 others; he was on the board of the Brandon Corporation and the First National Bank of Greenville, the Liberty Life Insurance Company and the Greenville News-Piedmont Newspaper.

Sirrine was responsible for some 114 commissions between 1903 and 1932, and, like Lockwood, Greene and Co., each of Sirrine's commissions often involved many buildings (100 operatives' houses in Chester (1917); 25 operatives' houses in Laurens (1917); 100 residences in Rock Hill (1919); 132 more houses in Honea Path (1922) and 190 houses for Duncan Mills in Greenville (1923). In addition to mills and mill housing, both Lockwood, Greene and Co. and Sirrine designed schools, hospitals, commercial buildings, generating plants, churches and hotels.

**Defining the Architectural Profession:
A Brief Aside**

A Victorian novelist might pause at this point in the narrative and say, "Now, gentle reader, we come to an apparent discrepancy between the historical memoir by Charles Coker Wilson, a founder of the modern architectural profession in South Carolina, and the meticulously researched portrait of the profession by John E. Wells and Robert E. Dalton, late 20th century scholars."

Wells and Dalton list approximately 390 individuals and firms practicing in South Carolina between 1885 and 1935. Wilson, one of the preeminent architects of that period, appears to contradict this by saying "there were few architects in South Carolina in the last decade of the nineteenth century, and no work for the few.... The conditions of practice... were very bad; competition was keen among the architects of

---

[13] Wells and Dalton, 164-169.

the State and from surrounding states. There were few buildings on which architects were employed, and these few, in every case from the smallest residence to the State Capitol, invariably went through the process of competitive sketches from all architects who cared to submit them. The chief occupation of architects was the preparation or purchase of gaily colored pictures, and the winners were generally those showing in the foreground the finest team of horses and the gayest Gibson Girls."[14]

Wilson goes on to say that in 1912 there were only 37 architects practicing in the state. Put another way: he considered only about ten percent of the practitioners identified by Wells and Dalton to be bona fide architects. Wilson's criteria presumably included formal training or an apprenticeship in a reputable architectural office. The large, busy group identified by Wells and Dalton, but dismissed by Wilson, all advertised as architects, and most of them represent the extension or evolution of the old tradition of carpenters and builders (and in the 19th century, surveyors and engineers) who offered design services.

Charles Coker Wilson and the Creation of the AIA/SC

Portrait of Charles Coker Wilson
Artist unkown

Charles Coker Wilson (1864-1933), like many architects who came of age in the 19th century, was trained as a civil engineer. He received a C.E. degree from the South Carolina College in 1886 and worked for the Columbia, Newberry and Laurens and the Carolina Southern Railroads before opening an architectural office in Roanoke, Virginia, in 1891. He moved to Columbia in 1895 and for the next 38 years maintained one of the most active practices in the state. More than anyone else, Wilson molded the architectural profession in South Carolina in the early 20th century.

Working with various partners, Wilson's firms completed some 193 projects. Over the course of his career, he was associated with Henry Hartwell Huggins, William Augustus Edwards, Walter P. Tinsley, Arthur Hamby, Paul H. Youmans, James B. Urquhart, Edwin Douglas Sompayrac, John Carroll Johnson, Louis C. Darnett, James M. Green, Jr., Jesse W. Wessinger, George R. Berryman, Harold Tatum and J. Robie Kennedy.

---

[14] See "Profile of an Architect, Charles Coker Wilson," *Review of Architecture, South Carolina* (1963), no. 3, 23-29; also see Wells and Dalton, 209-219.

Wilson was especially known for the design of educational facilities, including Coppin Hall at Allen University, Columbia, the first master plan for the University of South Carolina and the designs for Davis Hall, LeConte College, Thornwell and Woodrow dormitories at USC. He also designed a whole campus for Meredith College in Raleigh, North Carolina, an administration building for Coker College in Hartsville, and more than 50 schools in North Carolina, South Carolina and Florida. Wilson also developed a reputation for commercial buildings; notable examples include the J.L. Coker and Company Department Store in Hartsville and the Palmetto Building in Columbia. The Palmetto Building (1912-1913) was steel-framed and 15 stories high – the tallest in the state when it opened. It was designed by Julius Harder of New York, and Wilson and Sompayrac served as supervising architects.

Wilson was a prominent participant in civic and professional affairs. He played a central role in each of the early attempts to elevate the architectural profession in South Carolina. Just before moving to Columbia (c. 1894), he had joined several other architects in an abortive attempt to organize a southeastern chapter of the American Institute of Architects. In 1901 he convened what was perhaps the first statewide meeting of architects; together they formed the South Carolina Association of Architects and elected Wilson president. The Association met for the next five or six years. It was a social success, but accomplished nothing concrete. (None of the Association's records survive.)

In January 1912, Wilson was instrumental in convening a meeting in Columbia which was attended by 34 architects, "every architect in the State save three" he later wrote. At this meeting the Association was reorganized, and the members endorsed a constitution, by-laws, standards of practice, ethics and a schedule of fees, all copied from the American Institute of Architects.

Wilson may have provided the AIA material, for in 1905 he had become the first South Carolinian elected to the national American Institute of Architects. By 1912, however, five more architects from South Carolina were also members of the AIA, and in 1913 this group of six formed the South Carolina Chapter of the American Institute of Architects with Charles Coker Wilson, president, E.V. Richards, vice president, J.D. Benson, secretary and treasurer, and charter members A.W. Todd, E.D. Sompayrac and D.C. Barbot.

The following year, the new AIA/SC invited all members of the older Association to join them, and from this point until the Depression, the AIA/SC grew slowly but steadily: there were 9 members in 1914; 15 members in 1916; 17 members in 1921; 31 members in 1923; 38

members in 1924, and then a drop to 28 members in 1928. As the AIA/SC grew, the older Association became moribund and withered away, its role co-opted by the newer, nationally affiliated AIA/SC.[15]

The national AIA was well established when the South Carolina chapter was created. The AIA had been founded in 1857. Richard Upjohn (1802-1878), a New York architect – and the only American member of the Royal Institute of British Architects – convened the initial meeting to create a local society, but architects from other cities expressed interest, and the new organization ambitiously altered its name to reflect a vision of national, rather than local, membership and service.[16]

In 1867 the New York-based AIA members created the first regional or local chapter, having amended the constitution (Article VII) to provide that "Members in any city and its suburbs may organize and maintain a Chapter of the Institute, having a President, a Treasurer, and a Secretary. Each Chapter shall hold two meetings in each month of the year, excepting June, July, August and September."[17] Local chapters soon organized in other cities: Baltimore, Chicago and Philadelphia (1869); Cincinnati (1870); Boston (1871); Albany (1874); Rhode Island (1875); San Francisco (1882); Washington, Detroit, Indiana and Central New York (1887). Clearly, architects found local and regional chapters to be constructive.

---

[15] There are several major sources for the early history of the chapter. To commemorate its 25th birthday, the chapter published a small volume containing three essays, one by Samuel Lapham covering the years 1690-1890; it meshed with an essay by Wilson covering the years 1890-1933, and this was followed by another essay by Lapham dealing with the period 1933-1938. This first history is very rare (I have never seen a copy), but these essays were published again in 1963 as part of an updated history by Walter Petty to mark the chapter's 50th anniversary. See: Walter F. Petty, *Architectural Practice in South Carolina, 1913-1963* (Columbia: The South Carolina Chapter, The American Institute of Architects, 1963). Petty wrote essays and compiled information covering the years 1938-1963. Petty's contribution is meticulously detailed, especially valuable for preserving a record of names, places and events. Describing records available to him as he set to work, he says: "Prior to 1953, the Chapter had been unable to afford a regular secretary or place for permanent files. As a consequence all the records were handled hand to hand, envelope to envelope and paper box to orange crate.... I have no doubt that much information and many items of interest have been lost due to this careless method of filing during the earlier years." Since Petty wrote, history has repeated itself, for the records of the last half-century are spotty. He said that he put his research in the chapter's files, but there is no trace of this material today.

[16] The British Royal Institute of Architects was established in 1834. In 1836 a group of American architects had attempted to create a similar body by founding the American Institution of Architects. Two of its founders, Thomas Ustick Walter and Alexander Jackson Davis, were among the early members of the 1857 AIA. The American Society of Civil Engineers and Architects was founded in 1852, but the professions diverged, and in 1869 this group dropped "Architects" from its title, leaving the AIA as major national representative of the architectural profession. See: Henry H. Saylor, *Journal of the American Institute of Architects*, *The AIA's First Hundred Years* (Washington, DC: The American Institute of Architects, 1957), 3-6.

[17] Saylor, 11-12.

Professional Licensing:
The State Board of Architectural Examiners, 1917

The early activities of the AIA/SC mirrored the experiences of other chapters as architects across the country came together to improve the profession. In the early 20th century, chapters focused on the need for professional standards of education, practice and construction. The Boston chapter, for example, was instrumental in creating the Massachusetts Building Code (1870), one the earliest in the country, and the Chicago and Illinois chapters successfully lobbied for the first state licensing law (1897).[18] Licensing became required in South Carolina in 1917, for with the endorsement and support of the AIA/SC, A.W. Todd, an architect serving in the legislature, helped pass Act 106 which established the State Board of Architectural Examiners (BAE).

It has been customary in the United States for the states to regulate activities affecting public health, safety and welfare. This state regulation often entails creating and monitoring professional standards of competence and conduct, and on February 17, 1917, the South Carolina General Assembly passed Act 106 creating the BAE to define the qualifications for the practice of architecture in the state, to administer examinations, maintain a register of licensed architects and monitor professional conduct. The original law provided that the BAE be composed of two professors of architecture or engineering and three practicing architects; members of the board were appointed by the governor to serve five-year terms.[19]

The original board was appointed by Governor Richard I. Manning for staggered terms and held its organizational meeting on May 30, 1917. Committees were appointed to draft rules, to prepare tentative examination questions and to report on educational standards which might be accepted in lieu of examinations. The first design test was entitled "A Jeweler's Store" and covered mathematics, analysis of stresses, physics, foundations, strength of materials, sanitation and heating and ventilation. On July 2, 1917, the board approved the issuance of certificates to architects practicing at the time registration was required

---

[18] Tony P. Wrenn, "A Purely Local Affair, A History of the AIA's Chapters." AIA Architect (October, 1999), 22-23.

[19] Until the mid 1980s the governor's appointments to the BAE were based on recommendations made by the AIA/SC and the sitting members of the BAE. It became customary to nominate and appoint new members from the regions of the state represented by retiring members. Members typically served two terms, and political affiliation was never a factor. In the mid 1980s, Governor Campbell informed members whose terms were expiring that they would not be reappointed; the AIA/SC was not asked to recommend nominees, and political affiliation became the major criteria for appointment.

by the new law. This first group demonstrated the early 20th century spread of development across the state, for architects based in Charleston were a distinct minority.[20] Seven of the initial licenses were held by architects based out of South Carolina; six by architects based in Charleston; six by architects based in Columbia; five by architects from Greenville; three by architects in Florence; two in Anderson; and one each by architects in Aiken, Orangeburg, Rock Hill, Greenwood, Summerville and Spartanburg.

In 1919, the handful of state architectural registration boards recognized problems posed by interstate practice and met to discuss formation of a national organization. South Carolina sent a representative to this conference and became a member of the resulting National Council of Architectural Registration Boards (NCARB). NCARB is currently comprised of boards from all of the states, the District of Columbia, Guam, Puerto Rico, the Virgin Islands and the Northern Marianas. The South Carolina Board has been an active participant in NCARB and has adopted NCARB recommendations within the limits of state law.

Today, the South Carolina BAE is a member of the Southern Conference (or Region) of the National Council of Architectural Registration Boards, one of six regions nationwide. The national council, consisting of all state boards and five territories, is located in Washington, DC. Its annual meeting is held in June, and the delegates set policy and direction by voting on resolutions brought by the NCARB Board of Directors, by individual regions or by states. Among its other functions, NCARB serves as a clearinghouse for architects and interns

---

[20] The most reliable record of early licenses issued by the BAE is an index card file in the South Carolina Department of Archives and History. From the beginning, July 2, 1917, the licenses appear to have been numbered sequentially, and numbers 1-47 appear to have been issued in 1917 (not all the cards are dated). The architects in this first "class", their license numbers and, when recorded, places of business are as follows: L.A. Clark, Charleston, no. 1; Frank J. Collins, Spartanburg, no. 2; Henry S. Burden, Summerville, no. 3; N. Gaillard Walker, Fort Myers, Florida, no. 4; John D. Newcomer, Charleston, no. 5; Henry F. Walker, no. 6; John E. Summer, Atlanta, no. 7; James C. Hemphill, Greenwood, no. 8; James D. Benson, Charleston, no. 9; D.C. Barbot, Charleston, no. 10; Thomas White Cothran, Shelby, N.C.., no. 11; M.F. Wittaker, Orangeburg, no. 12; G.L. Preacher, Atlanta, no. 13; David B. Hyer, Charleston, no. 14; Elliot R. Mitchell, Rockaway, N.Y., no. 15; W.H. Smith, no. 16; E.O. Sompayrac, no. 17; George E. Lafaye, Columbia, no. 18; William Sayward, Jr., Atlanta, no. 19; J.H. Johnson, Aiken, no. 20; Gadsden C. Sayre, Anderson, no. 21; Julian S. Starr, Lancaster, no. 22; H.D. Harrall, Bennettsville, no. 23; James B. Urquhart, Columbia, no. 24; J. Carroll Johnson, Columbia, no. 25; Arthur W. Hamby, Columbia, no. 26; R.C. Todd, no. 27; A.W. Todd, no. 28; Albert Simons, Charleston, no. 29; James Baldwin, Jr., no. 30; A.D. Gilchrist, Rock Hill, no. 31; James H. Sams, Columbia, 32; J.H. Casey, Anderson, no. 33; Charles W. Fant, Anderson, no. 34; John James Baldwin, Washington, D.C., no. 35; Charles C. Wilson, Columbia, no. 36; Olin H. Jones, Greenville, no. 37; F.H. Cunningham, Greenville, no. 38; G.E. Shand, no. 39; Rudolph E. Lee, Greenville, no. 40; R.R. Deal, no. 41; D.G. Zeigler, no. 42; Joseph E. Sirrine, Greenville, 43; William J. Wilkins, Florence, no. 44; F.V. Hopkins, Florence, no. 45; L.M. Hicks, Florence, no. 46; Walter D. Harper, Florence, no. 47.

seeking to be licensed in other states. (For an annual fee, NCARB will maintain an individual's records and send them as directed to various state boards).

The evolution of the profession within the state and nation has required changes in licensing requirements and procedures. For example, in 1965, the BAE first administered the uniform national exam developed by NCARB; this exam was significantly updated in 1983, and the BAE adopted the new version. Nine divisions are included in the exam: pre-design, site design, building design, structural general, structural lateral forces, structural long span, mechanical/plumbing/electrical/life safety, materials and methods, and construction documents.

As amended, Act 106 provides that it is a misdemeanor to practice architecture or use the title "architect" without being registered. Violation may result in penalties of not less than $100 nor more than $1000 and/or imprisonment for not less than 30 days nor more than six months. Violators have been prosecuted, fined and imprisoned.

Since 1917 the BAE has continued its efforts to protect the public by improving its standards and procedures as the profession evolves. A current concern of state registration boards is the need to ensure that registered architects maintain their competence by keeping current with advances in the theory and practice of architecture. Through NCARB, the state boards are developing a systematic program of ongoing professional development. To this end, the South Carolina BAE has sponsored workshops for building officials (1999, 2000, 2001), a workshop on ethical architectural practice (2000) and a seminar on the new International Building Code for state employees who work in design and construction. Without exception, the workshops have been successful, and participants have urged the BAE to continue sponsoring them. The board members and administrator (BAE is funded by licensing and registration fees; it receives no state appropriation) speak annually to architecture students about the pathway to becoming an architect and the legal and institutional frameworks which form a vital part of the professional environment. The board is increasingly interested in the quality of the three-year internship which is one prerequisite for obtaining a license. It is the conviction of the BAE that the internship should be more closely monitored and evaluated, and they are considering ways to make the internship in South Carolina a model for the nation.

In addition to supporting the creation of the licensing requirement and subsequently sustaining the BAE, the AIA/SC also played a primary role in the passage of a School Building Code (1923) and the first comprehensive State Building Code (1932-1933).

Until the late 1920s, the chapter grew steadily. By 1923, there were 31 members, 23 of whom were also members of the AIA. That year the chapter president, J.D. Newcomer, attended the national AIA convention and carried the banner of the South Carolina Chapter in a ceremony featuring flags from all the chapters.

Photograph by Alt Lee, Inc.

This AIA/SC banner, designed by Albert Simons; now hangs in the chapter office.

The Great Depression and the Historic American Buildings Survey

Just before the Great Depression, the chapter was wracked by controversy. Petty tiptoes around the issues and says nothing, but Thomas Harmon recalled: "The incident that helped the break-up was in the summer of 1928. I worked at Lafaye's office. I was working on the municipal auditorium [the Columbia Township Auditorium] just sketches – preliminaries. I later learned that it was a competition. All of the architects had agreed to have a competition. By the time they got things all worked up to have the competition, Lafaye had done the preliminaries, gotten the job and was making working drawings. That was the sum of the whole thing; none of these architects were speaking to each other."[21]

Only 6 members attended the annual meeting in 1930. Robert D. Kohn, president of the AIA, and F.O. Adams, an AIA regional director, joined them to participate in a discussion about the dispute which had

---

[21] Interview, Harlan McClure with Thomas Harmon, February 12, 1981. All interviews cited hereafter are found in full in the Task Force files in the Clemson University Archives.

arisen among chapter members. The "following year the chapter received a further blow ... by the discovery of the loss of the chapter funds."[22] After deliberation (again, there is no record) the roll was "reduced to 11 members and one associate in good standing."[23]

The tide turned for the chapter in 1933. Although there was no spring meeting that year, chapter members participated in drafting the first statewide comprehensive building code. As the year came to an end, Albert Simons, then president of the chapter, was one of four architects appointed by the U.S. Secretary of the Interior as a "collaborator at large on the Historic American Building Survey (HABS). The HABS requested the South Carolina chapter to select a district officer to organize and manage the survey within the territory of the chapter and by telegraphic vote the chapter selected Samuel Lapham, its secretary (and Simons' partner), as district officer No. 13 (South Carolina)."[24] Twenty-three architects and draftsmen were employed in this initial statewide recording of historic buildings. These surveys were important, for they provided employment during the Depression, brought architects together and helped make the profession and the public at large aware of the significance of older buildings, context and the sense of place.

This early HABS work provided the foundation for the National Register of Historic Places and later federal programs related to historic structures. "So successful were the initial returns from the first six-months project that it continued actively until it came to a long halt in 1941 with the ominous threat of World War II. By that time more than 23,765 sheets of measured drawings, and 25,357 photographic negatives of some 6,389 structures had been recorded."[25]

Albert Simons "was advanced to fellowship at the national convention of 1934, his nomination having been proposed by fellows in some of the larger chapters who recognized the significance of his work and influence. He was also selected by the federal authorities to be chief architectural supervisor for the Federal Housing Administration for South Carolina."[26]

---

[22] Petty, 13.

[23] Petty, 15.

[24] Petty, 18.

[25] Albert Rains and Laurance G. Henderson, *With Heritage so Rich* (New York: Random House, 1966), 139, from "Death Mask or Living Image?" a chapter by Helen Duprey Bullock.

[26] Petty, 18.

Iron Gates Wrought in 1823, St. John's Lutheran Church, Charleston
Drawn by Albert Simons
Courtesy of the South Caroliniana Library, University of South Carolina

People who savor cityscapes treasure Charleston, and everyone who does should remember Albert Simons and his co-workers with gratitude. Few American cities – or cities anywhere for that matter – can match Charleston's architectural reputation. John Ruskin wrote that "the greatest glory of a building ... is in its age, and in that deep sense of voicefulness, of stern watching, of mysterious sympathy, nay, even of approval or condemnation, which we feel in walls that have long been washed by the passing waves of humanity."[27] The patina of antiquity is pervasive in Charleston, but Charleston also offers a human scale, pedestrian activity, a benign climate and lush vegetation, a diverse population, glinting harbor views and historic details; these all combine to evoke a sense of history and place.

In his vivid book about historic preservation in Charleston, Robert Weyeneth says Albert Simons was " arguably the most important figure in the early preservation movement whose role continued into the Post War years."[28] In architectural practice and philosophical outlook, Simons held the past and present in an harmonious balance. He wrote "in our present day quest for progress and modernity, which is altogether to be commended, let us not ignore the value of [our] great heritage, which is far more valuable than mere pedantry, more vital than mere sentiment; it is nothing less than the spiritual record of a people."[29] He sensed the sweep of history embodied in old – and often dilapidated – buildings. Commenting, for example, on the sale of antique architectural molding, paneling and details from the W.B. Burrows House (1772-1774), he wrote, "the fate of the Burrows House does not epitomize the history of Charleston between the Revolution and the Confederate War, but the parallel is suggestive."[30] Or again: "It distresses me painfully to see our fine old building[s] torn down and their contents wrecked or what is more humiliating sold to aliens and shipped away to enrich some other community more appreciative of such things than ourselves."[31]

---

[27] John Ruskin, *The Seven Lamps of Architecture* (London: George Allen, Sunnyside, Orpington, 1897), 339.

[28] Robert R. Weyeneth, *Historic Preservation for a Living City, Historic Charleston Foundation*, 1947-1997 (Columbia: University of South Carolina Press, 2000), 223.

[29] Albert Simons, "The Development of Charleston Architecture," reprinted from the *News and Courier* by the AIA/SC [no date, 4 pp.].

[30] Harriet P. and Albert Simons, "The William Burrows House of Charleston," *Winterthur Portfolio, iii* (1967), 172-203.

[31] Albert Simons to Mr. Rivers, May 8, 1928, quoted by Weyeneth, 6-7.

Fence and Wall for Miles Brewton House, Charleston, SC
Drawn by Albert Simons
Courtesy of the South Caroliniana Library, University of South Carolina

Entrance Hall of Horry House, Charleston
Drawn by Albert Simons
Courtesy of the South Caroliniana Library,
University of South Carolina

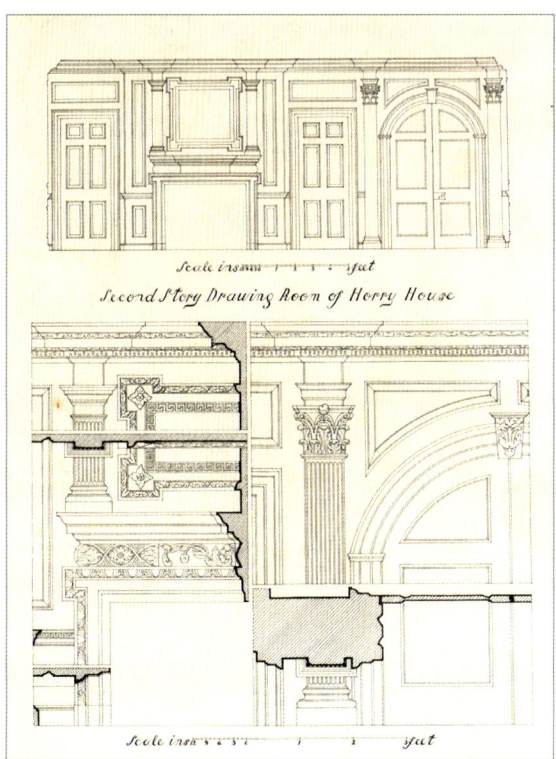

Second Story Drawing Room of Horry House,
Charleston
Drawn by Albert Simons
Courtesy of the South Caroliniana Library,
University of South Carolina

In addition to his pivotal role as a national director of HABS, he raised public awareness through sensitively illustrated publications.[32] He encouraged wealthy, influential clients to support the precedent-setting campaigns to save the Joseph Manigault House and the Heyward-Washington House. He worked with the planners, Morris Knowles of Pittsburgh, on the surveys and planning that led to the creation of the first preservation ordinance in the country (1931). Subsequently, as one of those administering the ordinance, he served on Charleston's Board of Architectural Review from 1931-1975. He was a founding member of the Historic Charleston Foundation and served as a trustee from 1947-1962. Finally, as a practicing architect, working with his partners (John M. Mitchell, James Hampden Small III, Dennis M. Donahue & Sam Lampham), he was responsible for many of the major restoration projects including the Dock Street Theater (restored 1935-1937), the Charleston Exchange (restored 1973-1976) and Charleston County Records Office, or Fireproof Building, one of Robert Mills' notable buildings.

Many people contributed in a variety of ways to the development of historic preservation in Charleston. And their work has borne fruit, for preservation here provided both a national model and the cornerstone of Charleston's modern economy. Whenever the movement is discussed anywhere, Albert Simons will be remembered as a key player, the indispensable man.

"Architecture as a Vocation"
By Charles Coker Wilson, c. 1930

C.C. Wilson at his desk

While the preservation movement was getting underway in Charleston, Charles Coker Wilson described architectural practice in South Carolina prior to World War II in a lecture at the University of South

---

[32] See, for example: Albert Simons and Samuel Lapham, eds., *The Early Architecture of Charleston* (New York: American Institute of Architects, 1927), or *Plantations of the Carolina Low Country*, by Samuel Gaillard Stoney, edited by Albert Simons and Samuel Lapham (Charleston: Carolina Art Association, 1938), or Albert Simons, "An Architectural Monograph, the Edwards-Smyth House, Charleston, South Carolina," *The White Pine Series* (New York: Russell F. Whitehead, 1928), XIV, no. 6, monograph 82.

Carolina. At the time, Wilson was at the pinnacle of his career. His essay is history in the first person, and much of it remains relevant today.[33]

"I take it that I am expected to speak with entire frankness on the condition of architectural practice and cannot, therefore, advise you to take up the study of architecture as a vocation if you are expecting an eager demand for your services or easy money. In normal times competition is keen and it requires constant vigilance and constant struggle to maintain a self-supporting practice; in depressions such as now prevails, architects are the first to suffer and the last to recover, and their suffering is not a 25% salary cut, but a reduction of 50% and even 100% in earnings.

"The normal volume of building in the United States is something more than $6,000,000,000, or roughly about $50.00 per capita. A large part of this is industrial work such as factories, warehouses and power plants, in which architects do not participate; an even larger part is in small residences costing less than $10,000, which are handled by speculative builders, mail order houses, published plans and no plans.

"That architects have little to do with building the homes of the masses is plainly evidenced from the commonplace and even shoddy appearance of most of the residential districts in all of our cities and towns.

"The estimate that architects handle 60% of all building work or $3,600,000,000 is more than liberal. There are about 12,000 architects in the country and this would mean an average of $300,000 of work for each, but a few eminent architects in the large cities command volumes of many millions and it is very doubtful if the average architect in the smaller cities and towns and the great majority in the large cities have an average practice of $200,000.

"Architects are generally paid a percentage on the cost of the buildings they handle. A very few, who have succeeded in making themselves the fashion, but not in South Carolina, charge 10%, 15% and even 20%; many others, and unfortunately they are not unknown in South Carolina, properly rate the value of their services very low and work for what they can get, sometimes as little as 3%. The American Institute of Architects advises 6% as a fair charge, and at this rate the architect with an average share of the work, or $200,000, with have a gross income of $12,000.

"If the $200,000 is on one, not too complicated building, and the client will allow time enough, the architect might do all his own

---

[33] Charles Coker Wilson, "Architecture as a Vocation," *Review of Architecture South Carolina* (1964), II, 23-24.

draughting and specifications one year and his supervision the next and thus make a gross of $6,000 a year, out of which he must pay for rent, typing, printing and office supplies amounting to about $1,200 a year and leaving him a net income of $4,800. But if his work consists of ten buildings averaging $20,000 and the clients demand prompt action, as they always do, he will need to employ three draughtsmen at a cost of $6,000 and his office expenses will increase to $2,000, leaving him a net of $4,000, provided there is no traveling expense.

"An architect handling $1,000,000 of the average run of buildings will have his whole time consumed in executive duties and in the supervision and coordination of the work of others, and will need to employ six or more draughtsmen besides inspectors, a specification writer and two or more engineering specialists, and only by the best business management can he hope to make out of his $60,000 fees a net of $10,000.

"The normal annual building in South Carolina is estimated at about $30,000,000, and about $18,000,000 is handled by architects. There are 44 registered architects in the state and 45 registered from other states, who get much of the cream of the work. As many of these non-resident are from New York City, with the prestige and financial influence which that carries and most of the others from the border cities of Savannah, Augusta, Asheville and Charlotte, they share the work of the state almost, if not quite, equally with the resident architects. It may be assumed, therefore, that 44 South Carolina architects handle about $9,000,000, or slightly more than $200,000 each.

"In the old days, even down to 50 years ago, architecture was a comparatively simple work, involving as now, the fine art of design and sound construction in masonry and in wood, all of which could be mastered by one mind. Since the introduction of steel and reinforced concrete, with the consequent high and complicated buildings and the invention of hundreds of mechanical and electrical devices with which the modern building is equipped, it has become very complex and technical work of a very wide range, quite beyond the grasp of any one man. It now requires the work of several specialists, with whom commissions must be divided or who must be carried on the architect's staff, and in any event adding heavily to the burden of expense. It is true that manufacturers offer this technical service free and many architects accept it, but it is interested service of doubtful value, and however concealed, its cost must eventually come from the architect's clients.

"The usual approach to the practice of architecture was through existing offices, as draughtsmen. Beginners get in normal times $15.00 to $20.00 per week, and in a year's time may advance to $30.00. As experience and skill are attained salaries increase according to speed, accuracy and talent to $40.00, $50.00, $60.00 and $75.00 per week, and in exceptional cases to $100.00.

"The week in architects' offices is usually 44 hours, 5 eight hour days and 4 hours on Saturday. Most of the public holidays are allowed and in some offices there is a two weeks' vacation on pay and a week's sick allowance. Some offices allow overtime at the regular rates, while others expect it in emergencies without extra pay.

"In order to practice architecture in South Carolina and in many other states it is necessary to stand an examination and thus secure registration, as in medicine, the law and the tonsorial art. To be eligible for this examination one must be 21 years old, of good moral character, a high school graduate and must have had 3 years' experience in an architect's office, but graduation from an accredited school of architecture is accepted as equivalent to two years' experience.

"The examination is comprehensive and searching and requires four days of intensive work. It covers the economic, functional and structural analysis of a building project; the art and science of planning, the art of design, draughtsmanship and the history of architecture; specification writing and estimating; the legal and business phases and ethics of practice, and the English language; the science of construction in masonry, reinforced concrete, steel and wood; mechanical equipment, plumbing, heating, ventilation, refrigeration, illumination and power. To pass this examination one must make an average grade of 75 and not less than 67 on any subject.

"However well-qualified one may be to practice architecture, he must be able to sell his services to the public, and the public is not only hardboiled but dense. It is accomplished with varying degrees of success by family and financial pull, by social contacts, by church influence, by secret societies, by golf, by playing politics, by direct and above board personal appeal. Very little work comes to the architect on his record or attainment. To most people architectural service is architectural service with little discrimination as to adequacy or quality; it is often bought like pig iron on a strictly price basis.

"Under the law of supply and demand there is no need for more architects in South Carolina, or in the United States, except to recruit the ranks as we die off, and it will require several more epidemics of malnutrition to create a real shortage. There is, however, a potential demand as yet undeveloped in the small house field. The magazine 'Fortune' in its January number discusses this question strikingly, and I quote a few sentences:

> They say the last frontier is gone. They say the age of expansion is over. It may be so. But there are other frontiers than the Rockies and other expansions than those across the plains.
>
> Mr. Ford discovered a whole empire westward of the $1,000 car.
>
> The frontiers today are frontiers of technology and price. And nowhere are they less advanced than in the building trades. If the building industry could build a good house to sell for $4,800 it would add 60% to its small house sales in the present market. If the building industry could build a good house to sell for $3,600.00 it would cross the present frontier and double its post-war output.

"If you think you can learn to build more economical, more efficient, more livable, more durable, more beautiful small houses and that you can convince the people, here is a real public need, a real opportunity for service and for profit.

"That need will undoubtedly be met, but without new blood in the ranks, it will be by others than architects. We are inevitably headed for mass production, for the factory built house – not the ready cut and bundled house that we have known for many years, and now sold on the installment plan all over the United States by a great mail order department store, but a house built and completely finished in the factory and shipped out in pre-jointed sections as large as can be transported and requiring for erection neither trowel nor saw nor axe. House factories will be built in every state, if not indeed in every county, thus minimizing the difficulties of long distance bulk transportation.[34]

"Brick and wood will largely disappear as home building materials are supplanted by light steel framing, pre-cast concrete slabs covered with linoleum for floors, non-corrosive metals insulated for walls; compressed fiber panels for partitions; metal plates insulated and covered with a wearing surface of roofs; plumbing pipes and fixtures built into complete bath rooms and kitchens in the shop; electric heat, light and power shop equipped. Such a house can be set up and connected to the public utilities in a week's time, and its total cost should be little more than half that of our present bungling, piece by piece method.

"But who will want to live in such a cramped packing box? It need not be cramped; the sectional method may be made quite as flexible and quite as expansive as the present small unit method.

---

[34] Residential construction has proven to be very conservative. Wilson's vision, shared by many over the years, remains unrealized.

"The deadly monotony! A real danger, but one which may be avoided. We are not now oppressed with any monotony in automobiles and none can fail to be impressed with their progressive improvement in beauty.

"If the movement has proper architectural direction, it can develop a greater variety and a vastly better variety than is now offered by the sickening display of wretched bungalows and row houses by which every town and city, even the great cities, are now disfigured. Whether we like it or not, it is coming and it behooves us to give it thought.

"From what has been said it must be evident that South Carolina does not need to educate more architects, but rather the better education of those of us with whom she is now afflicted. What she does need more than all else in this field is public education in the appreciation of architecture; courses of architecture in all the schools as a purely cultural study. For after all it is the people who really make architecture, who pay for it and who must endure it. South Carolina will not again have a worthy architecture until she develops better taste and exercises more discrimination than she has shown in the past 70 years."[35]

World War II, Hospitals and Schools, c. 1940-1955

The development of the architectural profession in South Carolina paused during World War II. Petty notes that "the last chapter meeting for the duration of the War ... held in Columbia during the spring of 1943," was sparsely attended, for "approximately eighty percent of the Chapter membership" was either in the armed services or doing defense related work.[36] Most architects recall the opportunity to travel; otherwise, they say military service did little to influence their practice. Robert I. (Bob) Upshur, for example, recalls: "I finished college in 1939 and my first job was in Sumter with a firm then named James and DuRant, currently James, DuRant, Matthews and Shelley. Jobs were hard to get then and the sort of salary you received required living in a home [as] almost a necessity. I believe my salary for some 15 months was $60 a month, not a week. I left that firm and from around 1940-42, I was on what we used to call defense work. Those were the days leading up to this country going into World War II, and I worked at Parris Island Marine Camp in Beaufort, SC, and in LeJeune, North Carolina, just as it was starting from nothing but farm land. I worked for architect/engineering firms and construction firms during this time."

---

[35] Wilson, 24.

[36] Petty, 34.

"In 1942, the draft board reached out their hooks and pulled me in. I went in as an enlisted man. I requested duty with the Corps of Engineers, thinking that would be my 'dish of tea' so to speak.... a friend sent me down to see the colonel in charge of the whole place [Fort Jackson], and I told him I thought the Corps of Engineers was what I was equipped for, so the next day I was sent out to the Air Force. Sounds like the Army. I spent a couple of years overseas in the European Theatre after a year in this country. In early 1946, after the war was over, I completed my architectural registration in North Carolina since I had started there before I went in service and became registered there. Of course, within a year, I requested and obtained reciprocation in South Carolina. In 1946, I moved to Columbia, and I believe I was the first draftsman hired by Bill Lyles and his partner, Bill Stork, the firm being known as Stork and Lyles. This firm was later the LBC&W firm, headed by Bill Lyles."[37]

The World War II experience of William G. Lyles was an exception to the rule. In a "Profile" in a 1964 issue of the *Review of Architecture, South Carolina* : "Lyles attributes much of his outlook to convictions formed during his five years of World War II service. At Fort Jackson at the age of 27 he was second in command of design and construction. From there he was transferred to Augusta in charge of selecting the site and designing Fort Gordon. And then to Washington as a junior officer on the General Staff. From there on the first boat of American troops to England. He served three and one-half years as head of Design and Engineering for the Chief Engineer of the European Theatre and returned after the war with his Colonel's eagles and a Legion of Merit. These experiences – particularly in Europe where he had opportunity to select and direct the best architectural and engineering talent that this country, France and England, could offer – gave him a profound respect for the 'boys from the South'. Their common sense and perseverance seemed more important than degrees and titles many times when the going was rough."[38]

The first post war chapter meeting was held in Columbia on January 8, 1946. There were 29 corporate members, and the balance in the treasury was $43.05.[39] The chapter quickly focused on issues raised by an unprecedented wave of hospital and school construction. In 1947 the federal Hill-Burton Act (P.L. 725) provided federal subsidies for

---

[37] Interview with Bob Upshur, typescript in the Task Force files.

[38] "Profile of William G. Lyles of Lyles, Bissett, Carlisle, and Wolff – Columbia," *Review of Architecture, South Carolina*, No. 1, 1964, 31.

[39] Petty, 36.

hospitals and other health care facilities. The chapter helped the state develop administrative guidelines required to participate in this federal program. The AIA/SC also provided information to its members about federal regulations and the complexities of modern hospital design.

It would be hard to over-emphasize the architectural impact of the Hill-Burton Act, for taken as a group, the hospitals were the most significant new building type in South Carolina since the coming of the textile mills at the turn of the century. Over a period of 15 years approximately $88 million dollars was spent to build 25 new hospitals, 58 hospital additions, 31 public health centers, 62 auxiliary health centers, 8 nurses residences, 4 nurses training schools, 8 chronic disease facilities, 11 diagnostic centers, 8 nursing homes and 3 rehabilitation centers.[40] Bill Stork and Harlan McClure recalled that literature distributed by the Duke Endowment helped South Carolina architects meet this challenge. [41]

Public schools, like hospitals, provided a new source of work in the Post War era.[42] In 1948 the director of the State School House Planning Division of the State Board of Education began a needs assessment of schools across the state. Since the Depression there had been little maintenance and less new construction. To make matters worse, for 30 years prior to World War II the Board of Education had promoted the use of stock, standardized plans which often proved ill suited to local needs. The chapter was successful in having the use of stock plans discontinued, and beginning in 1949, meetings were held for architects, educators and the State Educational Finance Commission. These meetings offered a national perspective on the school planning process and design details – lighting, furniture and the configuration of classrooms. The pent up demand which prompted these meetings was quickly evident: $210,646,000 was spent on school construction, 1951-1962.[43] This burst of funding was motivated in large measure to forestall racial integration by demonstrably providing separate but equal facilities.

---

[40] Petty, 44.

[41] Interview, Bill Stork, Harlan McClure, Dot Stork and an anonymous student, January 28, 1981.

[42] In 1940, Tom Harmon, as president of the Chapter, tried to address state policy concerning the design of schools. The issue spurred the formation of a State Association of Architects (with Harmon as president), but World War II overwhelmed all other concerns, and the association was not revived after the War.

[43] Petty, 49-51.

Architectural Education: Rudolph Edward (Pop) Lee

Charles Coker Wilson molded professional life in the early 20th century. Pop Lee, and after him Harlan McClure, shaped the curriculum at Clemson which molded many of the architects.

Rudolph Edward Lee
Courtesy of Clemson
University Archives

Rudolph Edward Lee was born in Anderson, SC, attended the Citadel briefly, transferred to Clemson and was a member of the first graduating class in engineering (1896). His professional life was subsequently intertwined with the development of the architectural curriculum.[44] Upon graduating as an electrical and mechanical engineer, Lee was hired as a mathematics tutor by Clemson in 1896. He left for several years to study at the Zanerian Art School (Columbus, Ohio) in 1899, Cornell (1900) and the University of Pennsylvania (1901). He returned and taught as an associate professor of architecture and drawing, 1900-1912. In March 1912, he became a full professor of drawing and designing and de facto head of a new constellation of courses in the engineering department. Taken as a sequence, the courses offered a four-year course of study called Architectural Engineering.

The 1911-1912 Clemson catalogue noted: "This course is established to comply with an increasing demand in the south for men trained in architectural design, building construction, and allied subjects.... It is recognized that architecture must be treated as an art as well as a science and as drawing and design are most essential elements in an architect's professional work, the greatest possible amount of time is given to them in the junior and senior years." Subsequent catalogues indicate there were two graduates in 1915 and three more in 1916.

The new architectural curriculum appears to have been a direct outgrowth of Lee's training and interests. First as a faculty member and then as College Architect, he was responsible, as an associate with W.M. Riggs, for third barracks (1907), the Alumni Association Clubhouse (1908), an addition to the engineering building (1908), dairy buildings and professors' residences (1911-1912), the YMCA building (1915), enlarging the college auditorium (1924), the conversion of the agricultural building into a college library (1925), the design of Riggs Hall of Engineering and Architecture (1927), and the field house (1929). In addition to teaching and working on campus, Lee maintained a

---

[44] For a brief biography of Pop Lee (1876-1959), see Wells and Dalton, 102-104.

significant private practice, designing schools in Pendleton, Arkwright, Marion, Wilkinsville, Greenville, and Landrum. He was an active participant in professional affairs and is probably responsible for establishing the precedent that the architectural faculty at Clemson should be members of the AIA. In 1917, he was appointed by the governor as a charter member of the new South Carolina Board of Architectural Examiners; he was on the BAE continuously until 1948 and served as chairman, 1933-1948.

Speaking of Clemson's architectural program under Lee, Hugh Chapman recalls: "It was small, of course in 1935 when I started [at the] tail end of the Depression. There were about 30 people that started in architecture and wound up about 12 as I recall. Out of the 12, two transferred in, so you might say 10 out of the original 30 [completed the course]. I think it was an excellent school .... Now there [were] all sorts of cultural advantages ... that Clemson didn't have in its rural setting but I had a whole series of great teachers. Matter of fact one of them went on to head the school of fine arts at University of Oregon, another one went to Rice, another to University of Virginia.... That was another era. There wasn't much money and the school had one copy of Bannister Fletcher's *History of Architecture* and it was held together with rubber bands, and when you studied the *History of Architecture*, you took tracing paper and traced the drawings from that since you couldn't afford to buy a book. [All] that was probably the best thing that ever happened to me because I learned more ... that way than I would if I had money to buy the book. No, I think Clemson has long been a good school. At least it was a good school when I was there." [45]

Writing near the end of his career in the late 1940s, Lee noted that for two decades the architectural program had produced graduates of "good reputation and ability." He reminisced that the program was "born in an attic up between the roof trusses of the old mechanical hall" which burned in 1926. When Riggs Hall was completed, the architecture department moved into the top floor, but with enrollments growing, Lee

Pop Lee at his desk
Courtesy of Clemson University Archives

---

[45] Typescript by Carolyn Thomas of an interview with Hugh Chapman, September 30, 1981.

recalled "constantly searching for a space for another drafting table." And he knew that the program needed to grow: "In order to perfect our curriculum and keep in step with the modern trend, there are certain ideals toward which we should work. We now have a 5-year course in architecture and a 4-year course in architectural engineering and should have a 4-year course in city planning and in landscape architecture.... We are striving to rebuild our faculty; we have several good men, but need several more.... There should be at least one teacher of history, two or three in free-hand and color, and three or more in building construction, working drawings and the engineering subjects of mechanics, strength of materials, reinforced concrete and similar subjects.... The department should be divorced from the engineering school."[46]

Although he retired in 1948, Lee wrote Dr. R.F. Poole, president of Clemson (May 17, 1951) suggesting that the president and trustees consider "the matter of separating the architecture department from the school of engineering and forming a School of Architecture" because the "approach to a problem by the engineer is so different than that of the architect that the accrediting board of the Association of Collegiate Schools of Architecture and the American Institute of Architects have been active against that present type of organization." Lee pointed out that "four items [are] necessary for accrediting: 1) the formation of a School of Architecture; 2) appointment of an outstanding dean; 3) additional library books and supervision; 4) additional quarters."

During Lee's tenure, the architecture faculty grew slowly. Rosamond Walcott came to Clemson in 1918 from Cornell to teach architecture. "Those who were students in the 1940s," writes Earle Gaulden, "remember that Professor Andy Anderson taught design and D. Hodge taught watercolor and drawing while Lee was in charge of construction and specifications. Rudolph Lee was tall and slender and very quiet. He was not a social creature, despite the affectionate 'Pop,' and he delegated the task of working with students to Professor Anderson. It was the distinctive practice of the seniors to paint a silhouette of their heads below the cornice around the drafting rooms in Riggs Hall."[47]

Following Lee's retirement, John Gates took over as Head of the Department of Architecture, which remained a unit within the larger School of Engineering. Gates was a graduate of Yale's School of Architecture. Before coming to Clemson, he had designed a gymnasium for New York University, the Cove Neck Long Island Tennis Club, worked

---

[46] Quotes from documents by Lee are taken from a typescript by F. Earle Gaulden in the Task Force files.

[47] Gaulden, typescript.

as an architect for the State of Connecticut and been Supervisor of Government and War Housing in the Carolinas, a position which entailed the supervision of pre-fab housing for veterans on the Clemson campus.

Gates' administration took the department into the national Beaux Arts Institute, the dominant architectural education organization in America prior to World War II. The institute formulated and issued design problems to member schools and held a series of national design competitions. Its methods were based on the Ecole des Beaux Arts in France, and it was a conservative force in architectural education.[48] The Beaux Arts' instruction which Gates brought to Clemson enlarged the students' perspective, but the conservative bias of the Beaux Arts clashed with an influx of World War II veterans whose maturity and experience made the student body less provincial and perhaps less tractable.

The faculty grew during Gates tenure: Robert Longstreet and Gilmer Petroff were hired, as were George Means, a veteran and graduate of Case Western Reserve, and Joseph Young, who had graduated from the University of Texas. Despite financial constraints, new leadership and faculty, the presence of veterans as students and the construction of the Clemson House, all contributed to a sense of growth and change during the post war period.

Writing of these post war years, Homer Blackwell recalled: "I started at Clemson in the fall of 1947 and graduated in January, 30, 1950 with a B.S. in Architecture. I felt that I did not get a good architectural education, particularly as far as design was concerned. The head of the school at that time was not a top-notch administrator or architect; he was more of a mediocre architect – don't think he was even registered at that time.... I had some run-ins with him at the school about the quality of education, the way he ran the school. At one point in my senior year, I was ready to leave to go somewhere else, but one of my professors talked me into staying and I stayed on and finished up, but when I came out I had made up my mind that I was going to do everything I could to get rid of the head of the school and work to improve the quality of education at Clemson, and after talking to a few architects around the state, it was quite evident that they had the same thoughts so there was a group of architects that got together and set about to get rid of the dean of the department ... to get someone there that was qualified ... to really build up the quality of education at the architecture department at Clemson. That was started in 1954 and as well as I can remember, in 1955 after the

---

[48] Richard Morris Hunt, who enrolled in the Ecole des Beaux Arts in 1846, was the first American to formally study architecture in Europe. He returned to the United States in 1855. He used Beaux Arts methods to train apprentices in his New York office, and they, in turn, made Beaux Arts training the norm as academic architectural training began in post Civil War America.

committee was formed and working with the college and trustees, interviews were held for a new dean. The old dean was let go."[49]

An accrediting team (NAAB), chaired by Herbert Beckwith of M.I.T., had visited the Department of Architecture in 1954. Armed with their report, a group of AIA/SC members led by William C. Lyles convinced the Clemson trustees to seek a new dean and improve the program. Harlan E. McClure, a professor in the School of Architecture at the University of Minnesota, was chosen after an extensive national search. He arrived in August 1955.

A Synopsis of the McClure Era at Clemson, 1955-1983.

McClure quickly initiated major changes. He applied at once for a visit by an NAAB accreditation committee, and this was scheduled for the spring of 1956. The curriculum and studios were reorganized. The NAAB committee, Richard M. Bennett, FAIA, Albert Simons, FAIA, and Paul Heffernan, FAIA, were on campus for three days; their report was favorable, and the Clemson Department of Architecture became (for the first time) nationally accredited.

To sponsor special lectures, take field trips and expand the library, McClure found that the department needed flexible, non-state funds. In June 1956, during a lunch with Bill Lyles and W.E. (Jack) Freeman, McClure discussed these needs, and they each wrote a check to the department, agreeing that the department needed its own foundation. G. E. Lafaye was also dining at Clemson House that day, and Bill Lyles presented the idea to him; Lafaye joined them by contributing $500. That was the beginning of the Clemson Architectural Foundation (CAF).

The CAF galvanized broad-based, statewide support for architectural education at Clemson. Architects organized dinners around the state. Contractors, building material suppliers and financial institutions participated, for it was widely recognized that creating an excellent program at Clemson was critical to improving the quality of the built environment in South Carolina. The AIA/SC chapter, led by Bill Lyles, made a pledge to the CAF as part of its annual budget. This idea "had a strong group of advocates as well as a smaller group of people who were staunchly opposed to the concept. There was an annual debate on the subject at Chapter business meetings for several years before the CAF item in the budget became an accepted expenditure."[50]

---

[49] Homer Blackwell, interview, typescript in the Task Force files. Architects, like historians, know that our point of view influences what we see; consequently, people see things differently. Phelps Bultman remembers John Gates, who preceded Harlan McClure, as a reasonably effective and constructive educator. University administrators come and go as institutions evolve, so it is not surprising that Clemson wanted a new man for a new day.

[50] Gaulden, typescript in the Task Force files

The CAF has promoted the evolution from a Department of Architecture to an autonomous School and then a College of Architecture; by doing so, the CAF has contributed directly to "the development of excellence in architectural practice in South Carolina."[51]

The initial transition from a department located in the larger School of Engineering to an independent School of Architecture took place in 1958. The Dean of Engineering objected to the proposed reorganization, and "all corporate members of the SC Chapter of AIA, except one person, wrote individual letters to Dr. Poole, the college president, endorsing the proposed action. The college trustees voted overwhelmingly for the action, and architecture was off to a new life with the collaboration of the SC chapter."[52] McClure was appointed Dean of the new School of Architecture.

To ensure that the faculty possessed up-to-date, practical as well as theoretical knowledge, everyone teaching design full-time above the second year level was required to be registered and to be a member of the AIA/SC and other appropriate professional organizations.

During the 1960s, "an important historic milestone, of which Clemson University and the School of Architecture can be proud, was its management of racial integration. Harvey Gantt, an able black student in architecture, had completed two years at Iowa State University and applied for admission to Clemson. His academic transcript was very good and he was advised that a portfolio examination was also required of all transfer students. After the tumult that had occurred in Alabama with integration in that state, the admission procedure at Clemson went quietly and smoothly. All requirements were met and Harvey Gantt was accepted as the first black student in any previously white school in the state at any level. Harvey Gantt was an intelligent, hard-working student with a great deal of self-discipline and a quality much appreciated by his fellow students. He completed the Bachelor of Architecture degree at Clemson with honors. He later decided to pursue a graduate program at M.I.T. and, after its completion, received the Master in City and Regional Planning."[53]

Throughout the 1960s and 1970s the curriculum expanded. The visual arts, architectural history, building construction and management, urban planning and health care, each became the focus of a new constellation of courses. By 1971 four separate departments had crystallized within the College of Architecture. The Art Department,

---

[51] Gaulden.

[52] Gaulden.

[53] Gaulden, typescript in Task Force files.

originally headed by Tom McPeak, enrolled students from many majors. The Department of Building Construction and Management, which had been promoted by Bill Carlisle, FAIA, fostered a better understanding of the building industry.[54] The Department of City Planning and Urban Design was organized by Ed Falk and promoted an awareness of larger social issues. A group of courses focusing on health care, although never formally a department, was developed by George Means and introduced students to this increasingly important area of architectural practice.

The College of Architecture initially offered a 5-year Bachelor of Architecture degree. "After much study, this degree was replaced [in 1971] by the Master of Architecture degree program as envisioned in the Princeton report, called 'The 4 + 2', and Clemson was one of the first in the country" to adopt the expanded course of study.[55] The progress being made at Clemson was validated nationally in 1971, for Dean McClure was elected President of the National Architectural Accrediting Board and President of the Association of Collegiate Schools of Architecture.

The early 1970s were a time of optimism and expansion in higher education in America. In 1973, with the support of the CAF board, McClure accepted an invitation to lecture in Italy and, working with Cesare Fera, laid the foundation for the Clemson Center in Genoa. Pledges by AIA/SC members made it possible to acquire a villa in Genoa; a gift from Charles Daniel paid off the mortgage. The close relationship between the program at Clemson and the AIA/SC is personified by architectural faculty members who have served as presidents of the chapter: Joe Young (1971), Gayland Witherspoon (1987), and Lynn Craig (1995). A high percentage of the faculty are Fellows of the AIA, including Harlan McClure, Joe Young, George Means, Fritz Roth, and Jim Barker. Emeritus members include George Means, Joe Young, Emery Gunnin, Vernon Hodges, Hal Cooledge, Ken Russo, Peter Lee, George Polk, John Jacques and Gayland Witherspoon.

McClure retired as dean in 1983. He taught part-time and worked as a design consultant with LBC&W and Lockwood Greene. He designed the Jim Self house in Greenwood and an Episcopal church in Cherryville, North Carolina. One of his later works, designed in association with Lockwood Greene, was the School of Architecture building at Clemson. Harlan E. McClure died November 2, 2001.

---

[54] William A. Carlisle, FAIA, rendered distinguished service to the profession throughout his career. He served as president of AIA/SC in 1953; he was appointed to the BAE in 1968 and served two terms, then he served as a regional director of the AIA, 1972-1974 and subsequently held leadership positions in both NCARB (the National Council of Architectural Registration Boards) and NAAB (the National Architectural Accrediting Board). After retiring from active practice, he represented the State Development Board as project coordinator for the BMW plant.

[55] Gaulden, typescript in Task Force files.

Tillman Hall, Clemson University
Pen and ink drawing by Joe Young

The Piazza Grande, in Arezzo
Pen and ink drawing by Harlan McClure, FAIA

Chapter Two
Architectural Education in South Carolina, c. 1950-c.1981

By Harlan McClure, FAIA[56]

...The Architectural Department of Clemson College, in seeking accreditation was visited by a team representing the National Architectural Accrediting Board (NAAB) and chaired by Professor Herbert Beckwith of M. I. T. As a result of this visit and the findings of the committee, William C. Lyles, President of the Columbia firm of Lyles, Bisset, Carlisle and Wolff, and himself a Clemson graduate, became vitally concerned that the institution follow up on the recommendations of the NAAB team, and demanded that the institution relieve the then current head of the department in the College of Engineering, conduct a national search for a new head, and pursue such steps as he would recommend to build a quality program. William C. (Bill) Lyles vigorously followed through to assure that a search was undertaken. He became chairman of the committee of the AIA/SC chapter that collaborated with the college in the steps occasioned by the transition.

As a result of these measures, which resulted from the efforts of the AIA/SC chapter and particularly reinforced by the strength of Bill Lyles, a national search was held and Harlan McClure, Professor, School of Architecture, University of Minnesota was chosen, visited Clemson on two occasions, debated acceptance and on the recommendation of Professor Herbert Beckwith of M. I. T., and the efforts of the AIA/SC committee and its chairman, finally accepted the offer.

---

[56] What Charles Coker Wilson had done for the profession during the first half of the century, Harlan McClure did during the second half of the century: they set the stage for their respective eras. McClure's previously unpublished memoir was brought to our attention by Gayland Witherspoon and is published here with the permission of Susan McClure, wife of Harlan McClure. It is not clear exactly when the memoir was written, hence "c. 1981." It is history in the first person and should be preserved and widely read. The 88-page manuscript is in the Clemson archives. We have omitted several passages; deletions are indicated by ellipses. We moved several paragraphs to tighten the flow of the narrative and made a handful of grammatical corrections. With these exceptions, the essay appears as McClure wrote it.

The most important factor recommending coming to Clemson was the sincerity and dedication of the committee and the resolve of other members of the AIA/SC chapter at that time. Even those members who had gone elsewhere to school were committed to Clemson's improvement, and wished it to become a very good school. Moreover the economy of South Carolina was improving at that time, and the busy offices wanted to be able to employ South Carolinians with a strong education and with creative design skills. However, Clemson College at that time had a very weak budget, and the Department of Architecture, as a division of the School of Engineering had a very low salary scale and quite lean assets.

A bridge was needed to span the gap between the budget and the very real needs of a newly energized program. Since in the short run [the] formal school budget was inflexible, a means was needed to confront these needs and was necessarily external. After his acceptance of the Clemson appointment, McClure returned to Minnesota to complete his contract there, and simultaneously made a careful study of the existing Clemson architecture curricula, their sequence, and their coverage and depth. Certain objectives were established and preliminary phasing of their implementation sought in some aspects of the task. The existing Clemson architectural curricula were somewhat fragmented, and courses were combined, grouped and replaced as the occasion demanded. This provided a starting point. One warm June day in 1946, Bill Lyles, W. E. (Jack) Freeman, and Harlan McClure were having lunch at the Clemson House, and discussing the need for a foundation to help the then Department of Architecture; each wrote a preliminary check to the department and agreed that it should be to a formally established foundation. No sooner had that been done, than one of the state's well known architects came into the dining room, and took a table. Bill Lyles seized this opportunity, and we went over to the table of George E. Lafaye, Jr., and told him that we had just started the Clemson Architectural Foundation, and its vital need ____Clemson.[57] He reached in his pocket for his checkbook and made the fourth contribution of $500 to the CAF, which was thus firmly established. Another decision at that luncheon was to have a series of CAF fundraising luncheons or dinners in the major cities of the state. As a part of the new public relations activity of the AIA/SC chapter, Mr. Van Newman was retained as a public relations consultant by both the AIA and also the Clemson Architectural Foundation. Van Newman was a former newspaper man, and had a particular ability to pitch news articles [with] a special local

---

[57] Harlan McClure underlined blank spaces in his manuscript to indicate dates, people or things he could not recall; they appear here as he left them.

appeal when sent to the press in various places, having unusual success in getting architectural projects and school items published. He made effective use of local photographs ____students from the town as part of his efforts.

The intensive activity of the renewed AIA/SC in affairs of practice, publicity, education, fund-raising, and public service _____. The AIA also approached the matter of updating and standardizing the professional fee structure underlying services provided by chapter members. A booklet formulating a fee schedule was tentatively devised by a committee consisting of John Weems, Jack Freeman, and Bill Lyles, chairman. This effort included the study of professional expenditures on a broad group of jobs in a range of offices to accomplish each phase of projects in different functional categories. It was a complex undertaking aimed at devising a fee schedule adequate to enable the architectural firm to provide a quality service in the particular building category. After reaching the preliminary draft of this proposal, the State Budget and Control Board raised questions.... The committee made the continued point of seeking quality service which was presumably of equal interest to representatives of the state. It was argued that it was possible to provide a poorer service at a lower fee, but not the performance of a quality professional service. Thus, the chapter fee booklet was refined, published and accepted for several years.

The Department of Architecture, although initially a unit of the College of Engineering, functioned as independently as possible, and in matters of internal administration there was no problem, but changes in curriculum, the adding of new courses and the dropping of obstacle courses were subject to approval by the curriculum committee of the School of Engineering. While trying to develop courses and curricula on the cutting edge of development innovation was essential, and it was trying and even vexing to be obliged to explain every detail, and debate endlessly with a committee of engineers appointed by the Dean of Engineering. Wherever possible expedients such as grouping fragmentary courses as a temporary method of making necessary changes quickly without the trials and delay of the engineering curriculum committee [were used.]

As the Clemson Department of Architecture had never previously obtained full NAAB accreditation, this became an important first order of business for the newly appointed department head. Arriving in Clemson in August of 1955, he applied for a visit by a team of the NAAB during that academic year. This entailed a complete restructuring of the design studios before the NAAB visit to be held in the spring of 1956. The faculty turned to with vigor and approached the necessary changes in organization and structure with real enthusiasm. The NAAB chose a committee consisting of Richard M. Bennett, FAIA, chairman, of Chicago, Albert Simons, FAIA, of Simons and Lapham, Architects, Charleston, SC, and Paul Hefferman, FAIA, head of the Architectural School at Georgia Institute of Technology in Atlanta. The team knew that the South Carolina Chapter of the AIA had been deeply involved in measures leading to the search [and] selection of a new head, interim measures to help the new program financially, and the establishment of a supportive foundation (CAF). Albert Simons, FAIA, a practicing architect in Charleston, SC, and a prominent member of the AIA/SC had been selected as a member of the team, and [he] was most helpful.

In the department's effort to make excellence the goal in all work undertaken, quality was stimulated in design, and Mr. Van Newman, the chapter public relations consultant obtained publicity for the work which obtained prizes. A new spirit [was] generated and each student was required to keep a portfolio of his work, which was reviewed with faculty, and became a very useful asset when the students were involved in summer work interviews. By the time of the accrediting board team visit later that spring, student work was proudly exhibited by the students. The team spent three days at the school, and wrote a quite favorable report commending the program and the strength of its AIA/SC chapter support. Mr. Albert Simons stayed over the day after the team concluded its visit for conversation purposes and was invited by Ginnie McClure to their house for dinner at which he reported that the team had recommended a full accreditation for five years to NAAB.

The milestone of full accreditation having been assured, the department was off to a strong start, and the faculty spirit was very positive. An assembly of faculty and students was held, and a letter from the team read to the group amid the loud cheers of the entire assembly.

Several important policies were established as fundamental aspects of the school's character. The first was public service as a basic element of the school's being....

Philosophic considerations, such as assisting in upgrading the standards of architectural design and urban planning throughout the communities of the state were in themselves motives for "public service projects." In very short order such projects developed wide appeal in the communities of the state, and in addition to the educational advantages of such projects, they had wide public relations appeal as well.

As the statewide public relations appeal of public service projects grew, this vehicle was suitably utilized for contracts in other parts of the curriculum such as in historic preservation studies and preservation, land use, site planning, etc.

Fundamental to the reorganization of the architectural program and providing education of quality was the introduction of a visiting lecturer and critic schedule annually that would bring the best and most creative visitors to the school. These included international leaders in design, technology, the adjunct arts, urban planning, and professional practice. These visiting lecturers and critics were in residence for various lengths of time, varying from a single lecture to a period of an entire semester or a year. The CAF was important for the funding of many of these _____

The architectural program had set up a liaison with the education director of the national AIA, Mr. Walter Taylor of the Octagon in Washington. Mr. Taylor agree[d] to notify Harlan McClure of distinguished foreign professional visitors that AIA knew would be in this country, with the possibility of inviting them to visit Clemson as a lecturer or critic. This developed into a very productive technique for getting additional renowned visitors to enrich the school offering.

The careful selection of speakers not only provided the program with a new depth, it enabled a greater breadth in areas not normally covered in the academic offerings. As landscape design was not then included in the school's formal offerings, this deficiency could in the short run be filled by distinguished visitors such as Garrett Eckbo of California, Christopher Tunnard of New Haven, Connecticut, and Dan Kiley of Charlotte, Vermont. Longer-range plans envisioned adding permanent faculty with these professional skills, but the stimulation of creative speakers and critics was a very tangible asset.

The spirit of the school took on a very positive tone, coupled with an atmosphere of both collaboration and competition. Working with leaders in the fields was in itself a prideful asset, and gave the students a greater feeling of confidence....

Even the best of college or departmental budgets have the disadvantage of being fixed and relatively inflexible. In education as in business, opportunities present themselves from time to time and budgetary flexibility is an enormous asset in permitting a school to seize these unforeseen opportunities. As the CAF grew and developed, the great usefulness of flexible funds became more apparent....

Flexibility in the CAF budget enabled the administration of the developing programs to attract to the school distinguished visitors who were traveling in this region, but were unscheduled and could lend special richness to the offerings. In this way, Sir Peter Shepheard, who had been a friend and colleague of Harlan McClure in England came to this country to visit the University of Pennsylvania and was able to come to Clemson as well, through the use of unscheduled CAF funds.

As mentioned, active fundraising for the CAF was first among the architects themselves, and the by-laws of the foundation made the head of the Department of Architecture its secretary-treasurer. Early discussions amongst the leaders of the AIA chapter and CAF suggested that financial responsibility for the foundation should be shared by each segment of the building industry, as the CAF existed to serve the industry by providing better education for architects and other related divisions of the field.

The first formal venture in this fund-raising effort to include contractors, purveyors of building materials, and elements of building financing, was a series of banquets arranged in the major cities of the state, including Columbia, Charleston, Greenville, Spartanburg, Anderson, Sumter and Florence. The architects in each of these towns invited colleagues from the several branches of the building industry to a reception and banquet at which a program describing the urgent need for funds to provide aid to the architectural program at Clemson was a key point. The needs were delineated in considerable detail and made as appealing as possible. Various members of the local council spoke at these programs with general enthusiasm but with varying degrees of effectiveness. Some of the events were a great success in terms of the social occasion and because of the amount of money pledged on file cards distributed with a place for a signature....

The most successful CAF dinner was the one held in Columbia which had two hundred-fifty people present. At the summer meeting at Highlands, N.C., on June 22 and 23, it was announced that about $10,000 had been netted in Columbia after expenditures. Generally speaking the fundraising dinners had been an effective public relations venture, providing members of the building industry with information on the revitalization of the architectural program at Clemson and the external money needed to sustain this effort. However, these dinners took a great deal of time to organize, and had considerable overhead expenses, but showed the varying interest and effectiveness of the chapter architects in CAF assistance.

Interestingly, some architects in the South Carolina chapter that had gone elsewhere to school, were very understanding of the necessity to build an excellent Clemson program as a catalyst to upgrading the practice of architecture in the state. Thus every effort ... was made to have distinguished lecturers and critics at Clemson [and to include] these persons at programs of other councils of architects in the state if possible. It was considered desirable to have considerable publicity given to the lectures at Clemson, well in advance of the event, to enable architects from around the state to come to the event at Clemson, but also [to] make efforts to arrange satellite ... lectures. As most speakers were on a busy schedule [extending] their contracts did occur, but with difficulty.

Bill Lyles was the first leader in the SC chapter to see the central advantage in arranging a pledge to the CAF as an inherent part of the annual budget. Happily this idea had a strong group of advocates, as well as a group of people that were staunchly opposed to the concept. For several years there was an annual debate at the chapter business meeting when the budget for the next year was being discussed. In anticipation of this discussion, the foundation board and its strong supporters prepared carefully for these meetings, and were successively met with good outcomes.

The inclusion of a chapter pledge to the CAF in the annual budget after several years caused it to be taken for granted by the rank and file of the chapter, and this lent strength to the CAF financial status. The inclusion of a pledge of AIA/SC did not preclude individuals from making personal pledges, and many members did so with generosity. However a pledge from the chapter presented a central fiber, which made it easier to approach other branches of the building industry. The appeals to entrepreneurs was by necessity on an individual basis, and, although related to the general themes of the campaign, the particular approach was by necessity related to the needs and interests of that part of the building industry, and of course to the particular motivations of the company in question....

In 1955 close communication with several strong university faculties enabled Clemson to find strong candidates for the faculty to help in the struggle to upgrade the school in every particular. At the beginning of these endeavors, the institutional faculty at Clemson was quite motivated but more ingrown than desirable. Although only one new faculty position was available to the new head of the department for the first year, a capable person was found for that position, but new life was sought and found in the form of visiting lecturers and critics sponsored by the newly established Clemson Architectural Foundation. Visiting critics such as Buckminster Fuller, Dan Kiley, Richard Neutra and John Burchard stimulated the students, strengthened their morale, and helped them to seek excellence in all of their studies.

As modest increases in budget were found, several able practitioners in the area were induced to join the faculty on a part-time basis. These people took their classes to see their work in progress, and CAF started the practice of taking students on class-related field trips to learn important lessons on building sites. Soon, student trips to buildings both under construction and completed were a commonplace occurrence. These contacts helped the students have a feeling for the state of the profession in the state, the quality of offices and enabled many of them to get in touch with potential summer employment.

While it is true that quality in professional education cannot be achieved by resources alone, it can also be said that lack of resources makes achievement difficult if not impossible. At the time the direction of the school changed in 1955, the resources available to architecture education were inadequate, and while the program in architecture was a department of engineering there was no indication that the fiscal picture would greatly change. The establishment of a means of external funding was clearly necessary, and the founding of the CAF created the vehicle through which academic upgrading could occur.

Until the school was independent, new faculty positions had to be fought for and appointments usually justified by increases in enrollment, and great care was exercised to make the best possible choices. The first criterion was the quality of the individual, his place and nature of education, professional experience and portfolio. No candidate was appointed without a personal visit to the school and giving a public lecture which was [part of] the CAF series for that year. Thus faculty impressions of the visitors could be taken into account. Strength was sought in technology, and architectural and art history as well as in design, visual studies, and planning. Visiting critics were engaged in these areas as well. The existing professor of architectural history at Clemson in 1955 was St. Hubert, a Frenchman with a distinguished background and a strong accent which South Carolina students found difficult to understand. He retired in 1957, and returned to Normandy in France where his wife had purchased a salt-water farm for their retirement. A wide search was conducted with a range of applicants including candidates from England, the historic restoration of Williamsburg, Virginia, and several American universities. They each came to Clemson as speakers, sponsored by the Clemson Architectural Foundation. Their respective abilities as an architectural history lecturer were assessed, and other factors weighed …. The successful applicant was Harold Cooledge, who was a native of Atlanta, a Harvard graduate who was completing his doctorate at the University of Pennsylvania. Cooledge had been a member of the faculty of Georgia Tech, and an experienced lecturer and critic. His classes became well known, and several years later the university had funds made available for alumni professorships to help reward good teaching, and Harold Cooledge became one of the first …appointed to this rank.

One of the most extraordinary members of the faculty of the school in 1955 was Emery Gunnin who had been appointed acting head after the previous administrator had been dismissed, and a search was conducted for a new head of the Department of Architecture. Before World War II, Emery Gunnin had been a skilled young brick mason working for his father. During the war he had served in the Navy, and after discharge he had taken advantage of the G.I. Bill of Rights, and come to Clemson and studied architectural engineering. With a natural gift for mathematics and an unusual background in construction he became a gifted teacher and very concerned for the well being of every student. He did a remarkable job of keeping the architectural program together in very difficult interim period before the arrival of a new head. After his untimely death in 1969, the faculty of the school accorded him the honor of naming the architecture and arts history library the "Emery Gunnin Library." His contributions had been enormous and this was a fitting tribute.

While architecture was a department of engineering, the various courses in structure required of architects were taught by engineers and were the civil engineering courses taken by engineering students as well as architects. While some of the courses were well taught, some had only faint peripheral concern to potential architects. The basic problem in such courses was primary lack of concern with the ultimate choice of appropriate architectural systems for buildings and design of them. While under the engineering curriculum committee, necessary changes were very difficult.

It was believed that structural courses in the architectural curriculum be best managed by a new Department of Building Science and Management in the College of Architecture. Extensive interviews with architectural students revealed those faculty members in the College of Engineering considered by them the best teachers of structures. As the teaching load of architectural students represented a considerable percentage of all structural design courses taught, it was recommended that the two engineering structure teachers selected by honors architectural students be transferred to architecture and one new position for a structural professor approved. So after many years architecture could run its own program in structures and assure that this work dealt with the concepts of structural systems and choices between them in the light of economics, as well as the design of such systems.

The essential changes in the syllabus for structural courses made their content seem more relevant, and a new course taught by Emery Gunnin on concepts and systems generated great interest. Several continuing education courses were also conducted in this area for practicing professionals.

In the late 1960's a very creative structural engineer on the Harvard architectural faculty, active in the Association of Collegiate Schools of Architecture, was invited to Clemson as a structural lecturer and critic.

He reviewed the new Clemson structural sequence and offered many helpful suggestions. A Building Technology Committee was established in the school's committee structure. The members of this group were sent on a visit to Harvard, M.I.T., the University of Pennsylvania and Columbia to explore the architectural technology offerings of these institutions. These trips gave the committee members a more effective view of the nature and quality of the structural and climate-control offerings at those schools thought to excel in these areas. They were less impressed having visited the programs than they were before the trip, but had flattering comments about some of the actual teaching.

The Building Technology Committee summarized their conclusions in a report emphasizing their belief that technology courses for architects should clarify the advantages and disadvantages of different structural and mechanical systems in the light of the spatial design framework. Quite clearly the architect needed to be educated differently in these areas than the engineer. A well-educated architect needed to be able to make intelligent and economic choices of systems appropriate in given design situations. Although in professional life he would not be involved in structural or mechanical design except of the simple sort, he would be constantly involved in making choices between systems in the light of design and economic considerations. Thus, properly taught, these areas could be creative and of great importance. The student so taught would be motivated rather than bored!

While architecture was a part of the School of Engineering, students were nevertheless offered some instruction in freehand drawing, and one artist was retained on the faculty to offer this instruction. Although he was an able and creative person he had grown rather frustrated with attitudes towards art in the parent school and soon left to accept another position. As the Columbia Museum of Art had an able director, Dr. John R. Craft, he soon became an ally in our efforts to develop a strong art program in the architectural school.

After several discussions with Dr. Craft regarding the kind of a creative instructor needed, he suggested a young man from the University of Oregon art school who had been stationed in Columbia in the army and was teaching art in high school there. This was Bob Hunter whose explorations in the visual media were very impressive. He was engaged as an instructor in visual art and immediately began work in very inventive printmaking. Hunter found an old Washington Press in pieces on the floor of a storeroom in the college library. No one seemed to know where it had come from, but there were strong indications that those historic remains had once been the early press for the Pendleton Messenger. Hunter put the old press together, repairing and making replacements. It was lubricated, painted, and installed in a newly established printmaking studio in the architecture school. The press was immediately put to very productive creative use. Bob Hunter was involved in some quite original prints that were a large assemblage of smaller plates, forming fanciful end results. As the art faculty grew, members were encouraged to use their studios for their own creative production as well as instruction. The policy of letting the faculty do their own art work in situ paid dividends as the students were inspired by this creative enterprise.

As the program in visual arts grew in quality and students [were] motivated by the work of the faculty, it seemed time to add an able young sculptor to the ranks of the staff. When the Cranbrook Academy was established near Detroit, Michigan in the 1920's, Eliel Saarinen, the Finnish architect, was appointed its first director. He assembled an impressive faculty in the arts to commence graduate instruction in a very pleasant environment. Harlan McClure was on the ACSA Committee on Teacher-Training Seminars which decided to have these seminars each summer at Cranbrook Academy. In preparation for going to Cranbrook that summer, a letter had been sent to its director asking about names of able young sculptors seeking employment. In reply, he recommended John Acorn who was completing his MFA at Cranbrook and was in residence there with his wife Peggy. While at Cranbrook for the teacher seminar early that summer, McClure met John Acorn and his wife and saw his work and invited him to come to Clemson and meet the faculty. He accepted and was made head of the art department. He is not only a very productive artist who has had commissions for sculpture in all parts of the state, he also has been a very successful instructor, and his courses are popular with students in other colleges within the university.

Selective admissions, as an early objective in the revisions commenced in the program, was conceived as a method to reserve the places for those best qualified to use the instruction and facilities. This issue was faced by all architectural schools, indeed, faced by all collegiate curricula. On the national level, efforts were made to devise an architectural aptitude exam, and this idea seemed to have merit if an exam could be devised which properly evaluated architectural aptitude. After unilateral efforts by some of the individual schools, the ACSA approached the Educational Testing Service of Princeton, N.J., and after preliminary discussions with this organization entered in contract with them to devise a screening exam.

The architectural program at Clemson was one of the schools requiring this experimental exam as an element needed by applicants. The examination seemed to have a great deal of promise as a basic idea, but after using if for several years there seemed to be little correlation between the examination scores earned by applicants and their actual subsequent performance in the program. Many of the other schools requiring the exam had similar results and it passed out of vogue. This, of course, did not mean that an effective aptitude exam was not a good idea but simply that a satisfactory exam had not as yet been devised.

In lieu of an aptitude exam, a much more time consuming process was used in the architectural program at Clemson, which considered scores in the SAT exams, rank in high school class and transcripts of grades ... in addition, personal interviews were required.... Some students had virtually nothing to show, while others had imaginative offerings with excellent drawings and written material. Evaluation of these criteria was interesting. The portfolio was a positive (or negative) indication of graphic skill and creativity. SAT scores were a positive (or negative) indication of potential academic capability but secondary school grades were an index of motivation as contrasted with abstract potential. Thus, an unmotivated person could have great intelligence but an unfortunately unsatisfactory academic prognosis. Each of the factors considered was shown to have relative bearing on student outcome in the program....

As graduate programs were introduced in architecture, planning and fine arts, the architectural curriculum was revised to provide more general studies in the undergraduate portion of studies with the view of strengthening general education....

On the positive side, admission to architectural schools has become socially fashionable, and competition for acceptance at the better schools had meant that architectural schools have as a general trend enjoyed applicants with higher scores in the standard admissions exam with the supposition that this denotes better preparatory education. This seems to be true at Clemson at least, where during the decades from 1985-1995, applicants accepted for the college of architecture have had the highest SAT scores in the university.

Although collegiate education expresses high ideals, these are often but not always a fair representation of actual standards. In actuality, competition is keen between institutions to attract the best students, to amass the most effective faculty, and to obtain the most external resources in endowments, research contracts, grants and awards. Success in these acquisitions is considered in academic circles to say a good bit about the quality of an institution. History and tradition have considerable bearing on success in fund-raising, acquisition of excellent faculties and the quality of students attracted to the institution. Pride in one's school, and loyalty to it vary however.

Clemson, as an institution, has in a general sense inspired loyalty in most if its activities, even when it was very disadvantaged in an economic sense. In its early days Clemson men and later women too, had an *esprit de corps* that was noteworthy in the sports arena, in military combat, and in their pattern of giving, even when the region had not yet experienced economic revitalization. Graduates were traditionally loyal to Clemson and wanted very much to see its academic programs enjoy success....

The response of key leaders in the South Carolina chapter of the AIA to the needs of the Clemson school was a part of this feeling of loyalty, but support was actually far broader as some of the enthusiastic spirit was contributed by architects who had been educated elsewhere and in some cases were natives of another state or region. For this reason the emphasis in promoting the CAF and helping Clemson's progression from a Department of Architecture to an autonomous school and then to a College of Architecture had as its key the development of a strong school program as fundamental to the development of excellence in architectural practice in South Carolina.

Thus the school could be seen as a means to an end, that end being a better physical environment for all South Carolinians regardless of their place of education or origin. This gave chapter members a sense of being a fundamental part of growth, development and improvement. It was because of this essential feeling that a small organization in a small state could accomplish so much in a relatively short time.

On the very weekend that the Clemson Board of Trustees met in Columbia, SC and voted to create an independent School of Architecture with Harlan McClure as the first dean, he was also elected Secretary of the National Association of Collegiate Schools of Architecture. This upgrading of the status of architectural education had received the enthusiastic support of the AIA/SC chapter. It did not occur without a great deal of political groundwork having been laid. The head of the then Department of Architecture had written to the dean of engineering citing the reasons for the change of status to school and showing similar changes occurring in other good schools. Unfortunately the dean did not approve of the idea, wishing it to remain an engineering department. In consequence, all corporate members of the AIA/SC chapter, except one person, wrote individual letters to Dr. Poole, the college president, endorsing the proposed action, and enumerating many logical reasons supporting the idea. The president did not take action himself but referred it to the Board of Trustees. At the trustees meeting in Columbia to which McClure and key members of the AIA chapter were invited, the college trustees voted overwhelmingly for the action, and architecture was off to new life with the collaboration of the AIA/SC.

Mr. Charles Daniel, a Clemson Life Trustee, and a nationally known building contractor was not able to attend the meeting, but he was a strong supporter of the efforts to build a strong School of Architecture, which he had supported financially. The action by the trustees received considerable press throughout the state, and in national professional journals. The position of an independent school had many advantages, and made it much more efficient to develop innovative ideas and work toward quality educational improvements.

.... As the school strove for quality, the standards of entering students gradually improved. The addition of a department in the visual arts [was] made with the view of broadening and enriching the education of students in the school, but also helping the quality of a general education at Clemson. Courses in the history and appreciation of fine arts, and architectural history [were added]. Hal Cooledge [was hired] as Professor of Architectural History; he was a gifted lecturer; and Vernon Hodges [was also hired] a few years later. [They] caused courses [to be] team-taught [and] sought by students [in] other disciplines of the university....

As the CAF grew and developed, the support of the Association of General Contractors of the Carolinas (AGC) became stronger, and the SC Chapter of the AIA invited AGC officers to its meetings. Bill Carlisle of the AIA/SC chapter worked vigorously for better relations between architects and contractors and theorized that if the school had a program in building construction it would be an educational asset to the building industry and also generally strengthen the school. After considerable academic study by the architectural faculty the school reorganized its technological programs including a new curriculum in building construction in a newly established Department of Building Construction and Management. This became the third department in the school....

At Clemson courses in city planning and urban design had been offered since the reorganization of the school, and urban design had played an important role in the public service offerings facilitated by CAF. The design work conducted in the communities of the state had not only assisted the communities in the improvement of their environments, but had also helped their economies. A notable example of such public service in historic preservation and urban design was Beaufort, SC Soon after this project, the school, now upgraded to the stature of college, established a graduate degree program in city and regional planning and set up the fourth department in this area.

Although never established as a separate department, the school had evolved a strong program in health facilities design and planning. This series of studies came into being when Dr. Hall, the head of the state program in mental health, having heard of the school's public service projects visited the Dean of Architecture in Clemson. At this meeting he asked if a study could be made that summer for alterations to their Bull

in the Genoa area and elsewhere in Italy. Genoa was a city of an appropriate size, a major seaport of the Mediterranean, the seat of a good university and with a great deal of little known architectural and art richness.

Happily, Cesare Fera also knew a great deal about the Clemson architectural program as Clemson had invited him to come as a visiting critic to study an area of Hilton Head Island as the leader of a vertical studio studying the feasibility of what is now known as Harbor Town. This study had been suggested by Charles E. Fraser, the developer, as potentially a contrast with the other development of the island. Jokingly, Harlan McClure said it sounded as if he wanted an "Instant Portofino" and told him that we would have a Genovese visiting design professor that year who lived only a few miles from Portofino. The study was made and one of the vertical studios was directed by Cesare Fera.

The several design exercises produced by the Clemson teams presented the Sea Pines Corporation with some detailed studies of the possibilities of a commercial port by the sea with a yacht basin, retail shops, offices, housing and resort hotel facilities. The idea had promise, and the studio led by Fera had an Italian flavor with a particular special appeal. As a net result, an architectural firm was engaged by Sea Pines and the idea of an urban port node on Hilton Head Island was translated into a reality.

This visiting professorship at Clemson had acquainted Cesare Fera with the nature of its architectural school and the quality of its students. His knowledge of the school and the dean's description of the idea of finding housing for a graduate student [program] enabled him to focus collaboratively on the problem... About a dozen properties that were available and suitable were examined and carefully considered. Ginnie McClure was particularly helpful as she was able to bring the search up against several practical considerations. One particularly romantic property was known as "il paradiso." It had been occupied by the German commandant during the Nazi occupation of Genoa, had a large beautiful garden fountain and a loggia with magnificent frescoes. This property of museum-quality was available at an attractive price. Ginnie reminded us that the maintenance of the place would require a large staff, and that it was rather too grand for architectural student working occupancy. This was of course something that needed to be said and carefully considered.

The property that was finally tentatively selected and ultimately acquired was ... above the center of Genoa and overlooking its harbor. The building was of a size appropriate for use as a student center, on a bus line and in a controlled neighborhood with many great and handsome houses.

communities in urban design and planning were known and sought throughout the state. One of these studies had a remarkably positive constructive outcome.

In 1970, the mayor of Beaufort, SC, Henry Chambers, a graduate of the Clemson engineering school and currently president of the SC Concrete Masonry Association phoned the Dean of Architecture. As the SC Concrete Masonry Association was a long time member and supporter of the CAF, supporting an annual prize competition for students, he knew well of the public service project[s] which the foundation had been sponsoring. He wished a planning and urban design study to be made for the city of Beaufort.

This charming historic city on the Beaufort River was on the Intercoastal Waterway traveled by yachts and other vessels on their way to and from Florida.... At that time the noteworthy historic buildings of Beaufort were well known, such as the Lafayette House and St. Helena's Episcopal Church, but the waterfronts, once the scene of great commercial activity, had fallen into ... disrepair. Moreover, there was really only one good functioning motel in town and a great scarcity of good restaurants. All of this meant that there was at that time nothing in the way of dockage and amenities to induce a yachtsman to visit Beaufort.

In the agreement of the CAF [with] the College of Architecture and the City of Beaufort, a study [was] to be made of the planning and design potential of the town. The waterfront restoration and economic aspects of the town as well as aesthetic possibilities of the entire area seemed great. At the time, Lt. General ____, U.S. Army Ret., was the Executive Director of the Chamber of Commerce; he stated that if nobody started a good restaurant in Beaufort, he was very much inclined to be the entrepreneur. Regrettably he died the next year, but the ideas were catalytic.... The Beaufort, SC Planning and Redevelopment Project became a splendid transitional undertaking for that design studio under Dean Harlan McClure ... ably assisted by David Hutchinson, a visiting professor that year from the Greater London Council in England.

The students who embarked on the Beaufort study that year were a particularly gifted group and much motivated by the future that Beaufort had to offer. Hank Chambers, the mayor, was by profession an engineer with great ambitions for the city and motivated in getting his community and its Chamber of Commerce to find the modest sums necessary to embark on this urban design and historic preservation study of Beaufort by Clemson graduate students. The positive spirit started with him and like-minded people. Thus, in several ways the Beaufort project was graced. The mayor and officials of the town were very constructively inclined, the town itself had very strong amenities and great potential, and the student group undertaking the project was unusually gifted.

Academic arrangements were made to enable the graduate student group to spend several days a week in Beaufort during the first, information gathering phase of the project. As in most such studies, careful attention was given to public relations so that the general citizenry was kept advised and contributed their ideas to the project. With the academic completion of the third phase, a public meeting was held in the fellowship hall of a local church, and the students had the advantage of several rehearsals before bringing their drawing and models for presentation to Beaufort. The drawings were hung for public scrutiny before the meeting, but the detailed model was kept screened until the appropriate time when it could be brought out with full oral explanation and dramatic flourish.

The mayor had invited important government representatives from funding agencies in Washington, and so impressed were they with the enterprise and proposed solution that informal promises of funding were an encouraging outcome of the evening as well as the enthusiastic response of the hall full of townsfolk - the "clients."

After the positive outcome of the town meeting, the student team, with faculty leadership, made refinements to the presentation material which was amplified with a written text and published for the use of the town in accordance with the CAF contract. The town, having been assured of federal financial aid, was able to engage a landscape and planning professional, Robert Marvin, FASLA to undertake professional studies to translate the concept into working drawings for the accomplishment of the work on the waterfront and park.

Subsequently, entrepreneurs established a number of handsome establishments for dining on Bay Street in the waterfront area and elsewhere in town. Various shops and offices were attracted to this revitalized center and Beaufort developed in a constructive way....

As has been described, the College of Architecture had moved toward graduate study as the vehicle for professional study, not only for architecture but also for the other curricula in environmental design and construction. The dean and key members of the design faculty had seen the logic of having a center for a portion of that study abroad, and an opportunity to explore the possibilities of this idea presented itself in 1972-73.

Dean McClure, a past president of the National Association of Collegiate Schools of Architecture, and immediate past president of the National Architectural Accrediting Board was invited to be a guest lecturer at several Italian schools of architecture. The board of the CAF

The idea of rotating faculty to the center was conceived as a means of expanding the experience of faculty, giving the younger ones the stimulation of work and travel abroad. It was seen as a place to broaden the education of faculty as well as students, and indeed, study trips arranged for CAF members and the AIA/SC and their wives enabled them to experience the center and to learn pleasurably there. In the ten year period from 1976 to 1986, seven such travel programs were offered for CAF members, and in addition to the Genoa Center, these trips included visits to the Palladian villas in Veneto; the Cistercian abbeys in Provence; France, the Greek Islands, Athens and Delphi; English New Towns, London and the home counties; and the architectural masterpieces of Corbusier in France and Parisian study.

In the fundraising campaign to support the Genoa center, members of the CAF were generally very generous and the AIA/SC chapter in particular. Although Bill Lyles was in declining health at the time, he served as general chairman of the drive in which former SC Governor McNair actively participated as honorary chairman. A proposal was made to Mrs. Charles Daniel by a committee of Dr. Robert Edwards and Dr. Wright Bryan and Dean Harlan McClure. Mrs. Daniel very kindly responded with a very generous gift of $350,000. Thus, the bank note on the establishment was retired, and the place was appropriately christened "The Charles Daniel Center for Building Research and Urban Study." The efforts required to offer study tours for CAF members to the Daniel Center was not only a worthy continuing education offering but it gave donors an opportunity to participate in their Genoa creation.

Efforts had been made to include in graduate student groups sent to the Daniel Center each semester students in the visual arts and planning and building science as well as architecture. Their representation made for richer study groups and made collaborative studio efforts more balanced. Whenever possible student participants were given graduate assistantships, and were thus required to perform certain tasks at the center as well as be involved in their normal studies and travel.

Generally in collegiate education minimal opportunities are afforded for active collaboration between disciplines in the solution of problems. Particularly in complex environmental problems, solutions require collaborative efforts in real life, and opportunities of this sort are especially promising in a special place like the Daniel Center.

After twenty-five years of operating the Daniel Center we have found that, just as on the main campus, the chemistry of different groups of students varies considerably. The motives of the leaders of a particular group will have considerable bearing on the outcome of the activities, attitudes, and academic attainment of that group.

Street campus in Columbia. He was told that the matter would be studied to see if this could be undertaken.

Of the faculty members available for work that summer, George Means came to mind as having a very special interest and experience in health care planning. [He] had relevant experience in hospital planning in the Charlotte area. Means was available for employment that summer and enthusiastic about the idea, and a CAF contract for this study was prepared and an area of concentration within design studies had begun. George Means and his student team spent a great deal of the time that summer working with psychologists, physicians and psychometrics and other staff members on the best way to deliver mental health care to those who had been institutionalized.

It became clear that the redesign of the Bull Street campus in Columbia was not the central problem. Alternate methods of mental health care on a statewide basis were carefully considered, and it became clear to Dr. Hall and his staff that the problem needed to be given much more in-depth study. A second contract was arranged with the CAF for continuing work in the regular academic year, and a studio for continuing graduate study in health care planning was established.

The fact that through the College of Architecture the necessary time could be brought to bear on the complexities of mental health care delivery and the problems could be studied without preconceptions enabled innovative concepts to be considered. After several sequential study-contracts, a method of mental health care delivery known as "the village system" emerged. This technique was based on returning the patient from a malfunctioning institutional state to normal responsible self-care in a condition similar to the outside world, through a series of controlled and measured steps in an appropriate architectural environment.

The director and staff of the State Department of Mental Health were pleased with the village system and eager to see this experimental idea translated into a functional prototype to see if it could be a model for mental health care and [then implemented] on a regional basis in the state. As it was generally agreed that an expansion of mental health facilities was badly needed in South Carolina, after considerable debate and public relations effort, money was appropriated for a trial regional center village. An architectural firm was employed to take this idea into the next phase, and the models and drawing of the health care studio concepts were widely exhibited in Columbia and throughout the state.

Parallel with the implementation of the village system, the health care studio undertook other public service projects for hospital[s] ... and similar undertakings. Projects of assistance to cities and smaller

Genoa is served by an eastern autostrada running from Milano to Rome and similarly by the main railway line and is thus accessible from alternative transportation modes of auto, ship, rail and air.

Bill Geiger was president of the CAF the year that Harlan and Ginnie McClure had [gone] on the site selection [trip]. Upon their returning to Clemson, Geiger called a meeting of the CAF board of directors to receive their report and recommendation. The board tentatively approved the report, and asked the president Bill Geiger, the secretary-treasure Harlan McClure and the attorney for the board, Crosby Lewis of Columbia, to go to Genoa and make arrangements to consummate purchase of the property.

The CAF officers flew to Genoa in July 1973 and with the help of Cesare Fera entered into negotiations with the representatives of the owners, and … a Genovese attorney that the CAF was advised to engage…. The property had been left in trust to two daughters of the deceased owners, [and] the matter became complex as one of them lived in South America and was not on speaking terms with her Genovese sister. Having an attorney locally well-connected socially and quite experienced in international affairs was a great asset in these very complicated contractual arrangements.

[It was] a very trying week of very hot Italian summer weather worsened by the non air-conditioned and cramped offices of the attorneys representing the owners and the involved nature of the transactions. Fortunately, those… representing the CAF kept their spirits high. Crosby Lewis and Bill Geiger, who were representing the CAF officially but had their own busy practices at home to administer, were obliged to return to the states before negotiations were quite completed. Fortunately, the general outline of the agreement to purchase had been formulated by them, purchase price had been agreed upon, and the president had empowered the secretary-treasurer to consummate the signing of a contract to purchase when the purchase [price] and other matters of consequence had been finally agreed upon. These key issues were finally decided in what turned out to be another week, and papers were formally signed. The next issue for the CAF was to decide how to finance this new enterprise. [58]

With the agreement to purchase, the CAF also obtained … permission to immediately occupy the property located at Via Privata Piaggio, Genoa, Italy 16136. This was a necessary arrangement as the College of Architecture planned to send its first full group of students in

---

[58] To purchase the center, 13 architects became co-signers of the initial bank note in 1973 on behalf of the Clemson Architectural Foundation: Reid Barnes, AIA, Fred Ehni, AIA, Bill Geiger, AIA, Robert Kennedy, AIA, Frank Lucas, AIA, Bill Lyles, FAIA, Harlan McClure, FAIA, Don McElveen, PE, Pete McKellar, AIA, Sidney Stubbs, AIA, Lad Tankersley, AIA, Jim Thomas, AIA, and John Weems, AIA.

the new graduate curriculum to this center for the academic year that was to begin in late August.... This meant that much administrative work was required in a very short time frame. The first decision was to appoint Cesare Fera, professor and director of the center on a part time basis....

The CAF had immediately started a fundraising program to manage the financial aspects of the purchase and furnishing of the Genoa center. As plans called for the rotation of faculty to the new center, these personnel became part of the academic budget of the College of Architecture. It was envisioned that the costs of boarding the students at the center would be defrayed by the participants including both faculty and students. This would be based on the total cost of food, supplies, and villa servants per semester and then divided by the number of students and faculty involved. In the first year, 1973-74, this total amounted to about $1,200 a semester per participant for room and board. The objective was to make these costs as reasonable as possible so that the only additional cost of a graduate term abroad would be limited to the cost of transportation and personal expenditures.

For the initial years of the program, the secretary's salary was included in the total, which was reimbursed by the participants. This seemed unfair as these secretarial expenditures were borne by the academic budget on the home campus. When William Atcheley was appointed [Clemson's] president, he and his twelve-year-old son made a trip to Italy, were guests at the Clemson Architectural Foundation Center, and were very favorably impressed with the operation and work accomplished there. Upon their return, the dean approached the president about the logic of having the salary of the Genoa secretary included in the academic budget of the college. Dr. Atcheley agreed to this addition to the college budget and also later to a building maintenance item as the center was used for academic purposes and this was consistent with items included in the academic budget for buildings on the Clemson campus. These budget supplements greatly helped the economics of the overseas center.

The policy of using public service projects as the vehicle for design and urban studies was introduced in Genoa as had been the case in Clemson, with a great deal of public relations advantages resulting. Exhibitions of student projects did a great deal to help the reputation of the school in Genoa. Indeed, the taxi-drivers in the city all seem to know what the center is, and about the nature of the work of the students. The bureaucrats of the Genoa government have become familiar with the center and its function through the efforts of Cesare Fera, as well as articles which have appeared in the local press and the exhibitions of projects in public places in the city.

encouraged him to accept this Italian invitation and [to] expand the trip to explore the possibility of establishing a foreign center for College of Architecture graduate study. After detailed plans were made, Harlan McClure and his wife Ginnie flew to Italy in March of 1973 for these purposes.

The considerations related to location were very important in choosing the right place to site a study center. Also of paramount importance was the selection of the best person to direct such a program. The location needed to be in an urban center, preferably an important seaport, with a rich historic and cultural significance, and differing physically, economically and socially from most South Carolina cities....

Contacts with the American embassy in Rome revealed that the American consulate in Venice was scheduled for evacuation and the property was to be disposed of. An attempt was made to secure this facility for the Clemson College of Architecture, but Wake Forest University had managed to make previous arrangements.

This property was on the Grand Canal and adjacent to the Guggenheim Museum. The building was in good physical condition [however, the] cultural attractiveness of Venice, its world importance as a tourist center, quite expensive [living] and its atmosphere [were] not optimal for a serious graduate study center.

Pisa was another location seriously considered because of its location in Tuscany, the cooperation of the university there and its many cultural attractions. However, it seemed to have too little contemporary economic activity, with urban complexities that precluded it as the best choice to meet Clemson's foreign location needs. The college required involve[ment] in contemporary social and physical problems as well as historic study. Similar questions were raised regarding Lucca, also in Tuscany.

So many American schools of architecture and the arts had programs in Florence and Rome that these locations had serious drawbacks for a school that would have its own unique identity and special programs. The general Milano area had certain strong urban appeal. It had an optimal location with regard to travel to other European countries, was Italy's economic capital and possessed much cultural richness. Its great size was a disadvantage, and the expense of properties and living became a huge deterrent.

Cesare Fera, the talented Genovese architect and writer, had been a friend and colleague of the dean since 1952/3 when they were together at the Architectural Association in London, England. Knowing the basic reasons behind the trip to Italy, Fera helped a great deal with the search

One of the Clemson trustees, Buddy [Theodore] Thornhill, President of Charleston Oil Co., and his wife were especially helpful to lecturers sent down from Clemson to conduct the programs. They were houseguests at the Thornhill residence.

Subsequent review courses for the architectural registration examinations were held at periodic intervals in various places including Clemson, Sumter, Greenville, Columbia and Spartanburg. Those reviewing for the examinations found the review courses very helpful and especially those who had delayed taking the exams. In addition, over the years, other professional courses have been offered in planning, field sketching and history. These have appealed to different segments of the school's interest and have occurred both in Clemson and in other towns in the state. For many years, interest in planning was stimulated by the public service civic design projects conducted in various communities of the state.

Various statewide historic celebrations and such activities have involved the administration, faculty and students of the College of Architecture as contributors or in more centrally focused roles. One important South Carolina celebration was the tricentennial of the founding of the colony, which occurred in 1970. Students and faculty contributed to studies, publications and committees during that interesting year. Major exhibits of art and architecture were shown in Charleston, Columbia, and Greenville, and the College of Architecture was deeply involved in these presentations.

An important historic milestone of which South Carolinians can be very proud was its management of racial integration. Even such cities as the nation's capitol, Washington, D.C., had separate school facilities for black and white students until the administration of President Harry Truman. Of course, South Carolina as a southern state, had segregated education and other facilities until the matter was brought to a head in 1960.

Harvey Gantt, an able, black college student in architecture, had completed two years at Iowa State University and applied for admission to Clemson. His academic transcript was very good, and he was advised that a portfolio examination was also required of all transfer students as well as an interview with the dean. After the tumult that had occurred in Alabama, the press was in for a letdown when the

Harlan McClure with Harvey Gantt
Photograph courtesy of Clemson University Archives

The very first graduate group sent to the Daniel Center in 1973 was a talented, flexible and very motivated assembly. This was a good thing as the building to house this operation was in its initial condition. The original family dining room was to be used in the remodeled structure as studio spaces, and a new large dining space for the center was created out of what had been servants' rooms and related functions. The students' dining facility was provided in the interim in the large kitchen. The cook employed for that year was Mario, a Sicilian ship's cook who prepared an outstanding cuisine but had a few serious personal limitations. Dining in the kitchen, with Mario at the stove became a memorable experience. Mario was an old-fashioned cook who went to the market at the crack of dawn several times a week and took his student assistants with him.

During the course of studies of this first student group alteration were needed on the bedroom floor of the villa, the addition of a great deal more bathroom facilities, larger water heating, and so on. It became necessary to house the students elsewhere when this was accomplished. Accordingly, we found pensione accommodations within commuting distance. The participants slept at the pensione, temporarily, and took their meals and studied at the center. This routine was supplemented by field trips and free weekends.

The student group managed this rather complex life very happily and well and found considerable interest in Genovese construction techniques and a broader experience with the life and manners of the city. They acquired tents and camping gear and took pleasure in weekend trips to places of note in the general region.

The tradition was started of scheduling a longer free student trip of about two weeks which they scheduled themselves with faculty consultation, and culminated with a prepared report complete with drawings and other data. These trips had great educational value, and their reports were frequently of interesting quality. The reports were presented to the group as a whole, and they were much interested in each other's trips and accounts of their experiences. Each student was enabled in this way to have an opportunity to explore his or her own interests and share their findings with faculty and fellow students. As would be expected there were variations in the quality of writing and drawing, but each student gained not only from his own but his colleagues' experiences.

One of the most notable projects undertaken in terms of the interest aroused by the design solutions was accomplished in the third year of the Daniel Center under the direction of Jim Washburn. This involved a study of the Molo Vecchio, or Old Port, and it sought to repair the union of the old historic center and its waterfront which had been broken by the addition of an autostrada or elevated highway, which provided access to the urban core and a considerable number of port service buildings [which] had been added under and around it. These student efforts substituted a tube under the harbor for the elevated road and thus restored the historic link between the [city center] and the waterfront. The models and drawings for this project were very well done and were publicly displayed with great citizen interest.

Active engagement in group design projects and other studies, not only in the greater Genoa area, but also including field trips to notable modern and historic architecture in other towns, required flexible transportation to make the best use of time. Accordingly, first one Fiat van and then two, plus a sedan were acquired and helped solve this problem. By the means of in-house vehicles it was possible to make a trip after breakfast at the center, take bag lunches, do a very considerable amount of work and study, and return to the center in time for dinner. This was a great convenience, and although an unforeseen expense, thus added a great deal more efficiency to the study programs and was also an advantage in the purchase of food, supplies and other operational items.

An important adjunct to serious studies, particularly at upper and graduate levels, is ready access to books, reports, periodicals, and similar material. In our very first year of operation a basic library was quickly assembled from duplicates in the library at Clemson and from contributions of material by the dean and faculty. A considerable amount of material was purchased locally in Genoa and from the bookstore of the Royal Institute of Architects in London and the American Institute of Architects in Washington, D.C. Members of the AIA/SC and others contributed periodicals and various resources enabling a small beginning to grow to a library of reasonable size. Participants in the program were required to contribute copies of slides taken on field trips to build the collection of visual aids.

The secretary of the Daniel Center also served as the librarian and her room was in the facility core. The secretary was obliged by job description to be at least bi-lingual, and Italian, English and another language is now necessary. Over the years there have been several secretaries, but the current appointee Sylvia Carroll now serves not only as the secretary-librarian but also as general staff-administrator. Sylvia Carroll is married to one of our graduates who is a member of the architectural design staff of Renzo Piano, a well-known Genovese practicing architect who co-executed the Pompidou Center in Paris.

As may be imagined, the selection of personnel for the staff of the Daniel Center is a matter of considerable importance as there is a very

Photographs by Jim Thomas

Charles E. Daniel Center,
Genoa, Italy

admissions procedure at Clemson went quietly and smoothly. All requirements were met and Harvey Gantt was accepted as the first black student to be admitted to any previously white school in the state at any level.

The seeming ease of the integration at Clemson was the result of considerable advance work on the part of President Robert C. Edwards and in the architectural school. The president visited many state leaders and convinced them that integration was not only the proper road, but it was also inevitable. Alabama was used as a bad example of the other course of action which resulted in a bad name nationally and in eventual integration on top of it all. The result of Clemson's action was very positively received, but as a result of a picture in Life [magazine], a reactionary person let the air out of the tires on the Dean of Architecture's car. A great deal of the credit for the successful outcome of this historic step was the character of Harvey Gantt himself.

Harvey Gantt was intelligent, a hard working student with a great deal of self-discipline and a quality much appreciated by his fellow students - he had a great sense of humor. He completed the Bachelor of Architecture degree at Clemson with honor and accepted a position in the office of A. Gould Odell, FAIA in Charlotte. He decided to pursue a graduate program at M.I.T. and after its completion received the Master in City and Regional Planning. He returned to Charlotte, N.C. to engage in the balance of his architectural internship, was duly licensed as an architect, and opened his own office for the practice of [architecture and] planning in Charlotte.

It must also be said that Gantt's career branched out to include public offices. Concurrent with his practice, conducted with a partner Jeffery Huberman, he was elected to the Charlotte city council, and after several terms as a member of that body was elected the mayor of Charlotte in which capacity he served several years. He was nominated by the N.C. Democratic Party as a candidate for the United States Senate to run against Jesse Helms, the incumbent. Although he received strong support, he was defeated, but this has not terminated his active political life. In the meantime, Harvey Gantt and Huberman, his partner, continued in their practice of architecture and urban design and planning. Gantt has remained active in the North Carolina Democratic Party.

Another graduate from the late fifties, Bobby Washington, has been very involved in politics in Virginia while conducting an architectural practice in Norfolk in partnership with his brothers. His younger brother, also a Clemson alumnus in architecture, and his older brother, a Clemson graduate in engineering, are also partners in the firm. Bobby Washington was a Virginia state senator for a number of terms while conducting a diversified practice.

The first graduate of the school to be elected to the Clemson University Board of Trustees was Bill Geiger, and during his time as a member was very active, helping to promote the interests of the College of Architecture. A second alumnus to become a Clemson trustee was Allen Wood of Florence, who has a great deal of prestige in the Pee Dee region of the state and is a respected practitioner there.

As the College of Architecture at Clemson grew in prestige, the parallel advantages of more talented and able candidates for admission occurred, and graduates were sought by excellent and diversified offices in various parts of the country. The economy of South Carolina, although subject to the same variations as elsewhere in the country, was generally more robust than other areas, especially the northeast region. As a result of this phenomenon, when the construction industry was slower in some other areas than in South Carolina there was an in-migration of architects, educated and trained elsewhere. Thereby Clemson remained no longer the sole principal school for SC architects.

In the contemporary world of practice there is considerable demand in other regions for Clemson educated architects, and conversely the in-migration or those educated elsewhere has probably made for a healthy balance. These changes have not generally affected the loyalty of the South Carolina AIA Chapter to the CAF and other Clemson initiatives.

To maintain the continuing interest of the AIA/SC chapter in the Clemson School of Architecture, the faculty, young and old, have maintained a strong interest in the chapter. To promote this faculty interest and to assure that the faculty in architecture is involved in architecture on more than a "theoretical" basis, in the late 1950s the school established a policy of requiring the faculty involved in full time design teaching above second year to be registered architects and members of the AIA, or an equivalent extra-national professional organization. If planners or engineer or landscape architects they were expected to be members of their own professional organizations and appropriately registered professionals.

This policy did a very great deal to build a truly professional climate which seemed appropriate in a professional school, helped a great deal in public relations, and helped to strengthen the desire within the several organizations to assist in the support of education. It was also an appropriate recognition of the fact that the school would not have been recreated and strengthened to its present state were it not for the sponsorship and support that the school has enjoyed for nearly half a century.

Some other schools and colleges of architecture have had strong alumni support, but few if any have had such outstanding, continuous professional sponsorship....

close relationship between students, faculty, and staff. It is very necessary for members of the staff to be at least bilingual, and to be able to some degree to function in another of the positions in the event one is absent or ill. The housekeeper, Andriena, has been a very energetic, cheerful and enthusiastic key member of the staff. When repairs or other work are done in the center, Andriena can be counted on to be a literal clerk of the works and keep accurate records of these operations. Actually, when the cook has been absent or ill, Adriena has filled in these tasks as well as accomplishing her own work. She works endlessly.

In accordance with Italian law, employees must be hired on an annual basis, and other Italian government regulations must be followed regarding their hours, benefits, etc. Because of these mandatory regulations of staff employment, it has become desirable to provide summer short courses and other offerings during the holiday months outside of the regular semesters.

At various intervals, the parents of some student participants visit Genoa for short periods. They generally stay at a local hotel and are dinner guests of the center for which they pay in accordance with a schedule. These visits vary according to the number of participants in residence at that particular time. It has been necessary to require prearrangements but as might be expected, unscheduled visits of various sorts do occur from time to time. Sometimes these unscheduled visitors are from other universities or simply personal friends. It is perhaps pleasant but disruptive to the academic programs if these visits are not carefully scheduled in advance.

Dr. Benvenuto, dean of the architectural program at the University of Genoa, has become quite familiar with the Clemson Daniel Center and has collaborated in some joint academic and social ventures. These contacts have been mutually beneficial. The best of European architects, planners, artists and critics that had been lecturers and critics in the CAF sponsored schedule at Clemson have been pleased to serve for varying periods at the Daniel Center and have broadened its offerings. In addition there have been architectural professors and administrators from other schools traveling in Europe who have been invited to be guests at the center for shorter periods of time, and have been speakers, jurors or simply involved in informal discussions with the students and have given variation to the normal points of view.

To stimulate the progress of continuing education, the college had offered short courses of various sorts to be useful to different professional groups in its clientele. The first of these was conducted at the College of Charleston in 1955-56 for candidates for the SC Architectural Registration Exam. The material covered was the entire exam but with particular emphasis on design and building structures.

Chapter Three
Significant Developments,
c. 1963-2002

Highlighting things which have affected the profession over the past several decades, an observer might include mandatory accessibility for the handicapped, a new emphasis on historic preservation and contextual issues, education at Clemson after McClure, the equitable allocation of state architectural contracts and changes in drafting technologies – to name a few.

The Impact of F.H.A. Post War Housing

The construction of housing virtually halted during World War II, and as the war ended the federal government, through F.H.A. 608 low interest loans, sought to stimulate construction to meet pent up demand. Robert Lyles, president of Stevens & Wilkinson, recalls that "the F.H.A. programs provided a launching pad for LBC&W after the war."[59] Working with attorney Rudy Barnes, LBC&W was responsible for 65 million dollars worth of construction between 1947 and 1950, and most of it was F.H.A. financed housing. In that three-year period they created 5,128 residential units in Anderson, Atlanta, Charlotte, Charleston, Columbia, Camden, Asheville, Augusta, Florence, Gastonia, Clemson and San Juan. Their multi-story residential buildings – the Clemson House, Claire Towers and Cornell Arms in Columbia, the Darlington Apartments in Atlanta and the Sergeant Jasper building in Charleston – represented a new building type in many communities. LBC&W emerged from the post war housing boom as one of the largest, most successful architectural firms in the southeast.

Local Councils and Sections

In the mid 1950s, architects in South Carolina began to promote collegial relationships with their peers by organizing locally based Councils of Architects. These groups typically met monthly or twice a month. They sponsored social events and presentations by building officials, developers and others whose work was of interest to architects.

---

[59] "... the office is organized with Mr. W.G. Lyles in charge of administration; Mr. L.M. Wolff in charge of design; Mr. T.J. Bissett responsible for the execution of working drawings and specifications; and Mr. W.A. Carlisle in charge of supervision of construction. Engineering is under the direction of Mr. Gilbert H. Rowe, Structural; Mr. Michael Centre, Electrical; and Mr. O'Leary Kearney, Mechanical." Anon., *Selections from the Work of William G. Lyles, Bissett, Carlisle & Wolff, Architects-Engineers* (privately printed, 1950), n.p.

The wives of members organized Women's Auxiliary Councils and did much of the work associated with the social functions, raised money, initiated public education projects and made substantial contributions to the beginning of a statewide historic preservation movement. The councils, which existed in Charleston, Greenville, Columbia and Hilton Head Island, were not affiliated with the AIA; nonetheless, they proved an effective means of promoting a sense of camaraderie among architects. In the 1970s, the councils were put on a more formal footing as Sections of the AIA.

The Greenville Council of Architects has provided the following synoptic history, and anecdotal information about other councils suggests that the Greenville experience is typical.

The Greenville Council started c. 1957 with Robert H. Longstreet, president, W.E. "Jack" Freeman, vice president, Mike McMillan, secretary and Charlie Liles, treasurer. Committee chairs or directors were: H. Harold Tarleton, social director, J.D. Beacham, professional director, Charles L. Potter, civic director and Avery W. Wood, public relations director. They stated their purpose as "the advancement of the architectural profession, the study of local problems allied with the profession, recommend policies or projects affording opportunity for cultural outlets, and promote better understanding among members of the profession." They met twice a month, once for lunch, initially in the basement of the Colonial Drug Store "in what is now the Pleasantburg Shopping Center" and once for a business meeting which was attended only by registered architects. The Greenville Council had an active Women's Auxiliary. "Architects' wives who had an interest in their husbands' profession formed this group. They had their own meetings and elected officials. Allen Freeman's mother was the first President."[60] Older architects recall that the auxiliaries became less active in the 1970s as women began to enter the professions.

Handicapped Access

In 1961, the American Standards Association issued specifications for making buildings accessible to and usable by physically handicapped people. The South Carolina Society for Crippled Children and Adults quickly lobbied for the adoption of these standards within the state, and the AIA/SC and the Association of General Contractors endorsed their efforts, including a bill which gave the standards the force of law in 1963. It was, according to the late Heyward McDonald, a Columbia attorney

---

[60] Typescript, "AIA Greenville: Forgotten Moments," Task Force files.

who deserves credit for its passage, "the first comprehensive piece of legislation throughout the nation specifically designed to meet the problem."[61]

The 50th Anniversary, 1963

On its 50th anniversary – 1963 – the chapter had 144 members. Reid Hearn was president, and it was a notable year. In the newsletter, Hearn pointed out that "this very important occasion in the annals of our Chapter must be given the fanfare it deserves. We are sure our Publicity Committee will handle this opportunity appropriately; however, this is March already."[62] The new president enlivened *Blueprint*, the newsletter, with whimsical drawings, wry humor and infectious enthusiasm.[63] He designed a rubber stamp and offered it to members: "for … stamping our mail, etc. (or branding women). Addy Stamp Works … @ $2.00 ea. They also have a new micropore stamp pad that's good for 200,000 (we counted them) sharp impressions without reinking". The magazine, which began in 1958, had a press run of 4,250 copies.

Invitation by Reid Hearn

To commemorate the 50th anniversary, Walter Petty wrote a history. In March, the chapter voted to spend $1,410 to print 600 copies, and Petty autographed and distributed copies at the fall meeting,

---

[61] "A Break Through the Architectural Barriers for the Handicapped," *Review of Architecture, South Carolina* (1963), No. 4, 32.

[62] South Carolina Chapter, the American Institute of Architects, Executive Committee Meeting, March 7, 1963, typescript minutes found in a notebook entitled *Hi Lites of My Year as S.C. A.I.A. President, 1963*, compiled by Reid Hearn, in the collection of Reid Hearn, III. The 1963 events and illustrations that follow are taken from this notebook.

[63] Many architects remember the elephants that romped, etc. through the *Blueprint* while Reid Hearn was ringmaster. Hearn himself wrote, "in answer to many inquiries – 'where'd you get those elephants?' – the versatile (sometimes morbid) pen of Heinrich Kley, late German illustrator." *Blueprint*, April 11, 1963. [This footnote answers one of the burning questions in the history of the graphic arts in South Carolina; having written it, the author is flushed with pride.]

October 19, 1963, at the Jefferson Hotel in Columbia. He also introduced a resolution, which was approved by the chapter, urging the AIA to save the historic stable and smoke house as part of the restoration of the Octagon. The chapter made donations to the work at the Octagon and to efforts to save the Ainsley Hall house in Columbia, which was designed by Robert Mills.

Henry Wright, national president of the AIA, came to Columbia, April 22, 1963, to present an AIA First Honor Award for the University of South Carolina Undergraduate Library, designed by Lyles, Bissett, Carlisle and Wolff, architects and Edward Durell Stone, associate architect.

That year W.G. Lyles, as chairman of the AIA/SC office practice committee, reached an agreement with the State Budget and Control Board on the text of a standard fee schedule booklet. (The use of a standard fee schedule was subsequently abandoned, for it was challenged as a restraint of trade.) Lyles was also appointed – as one of two architects – to the federal Government Services Administration review committee – an important body charged with monitoring all aspects of federal construction.

Historic Preservation

In historic preservation – another aspect of architecture affecting the quality of life - South Carolinians were the first to act. The National Historic Preservation Act was passed in 1966; it provided (and continues to provide) a legal foundation for federal historic preservation programs. More than 30 years earlier, however, Charleston had passed the first local historic preservation ordinance in the nation when it created its Board of Architectural Review in 1931.[64] The purposes and procedures embodied in the Charleston ordinance are echoed now in some 500 jurisdictions, coast to coast. Forty-one communities in South Carolina currently have provisions for historic preservation in their zoning and building-related ordinances.

Under Governor Robert McNair, the State Historic Preservation Act was made part of the SC Department of Archives and History (SCDAH). Charles Lee, then head of Archives, created an active statewide program which attained national recognition, and he was elected president of the National Conference of State Historic Preservation Officers. Within the Archives, Christie Z. Fant served as the first director of the historic preservation office. This office initiated surveys of historic resources,

---

[64] Albert Rains, *With Heritage so Rich* (New York: Random House, 1966), 46; also see William J. Murtagh, *Keeping Time, the History and Theory of Preservation in America* (Pittstown: Main Street Press, 1988), 103.

helped to fund restorations and assisted city planning efforts. The work of SCDAH helped people across the state celebrate and save the architectural heritage and thereby improve the quality of life in their communities. Abbeville and Chester, for example, benefited from early preservation plans. (The Abbeville plan was re-published by the National Park Service as a national exemplum.)[65] Opera houses have been saved in Newberry, Sumter and Chester; colonial era churches - St. James Santee, Pompion Hill, St. James Goose Creek, St. Thomas, St. Denis, Strawberry Chapel – have been restored; lighthouses, plantations, commercial buildings and residences, isolated structures and historic districts have been recorded, researched, and where appropriate – restored.

As one of the original colonies, South Carolina has a rich architectural heritage, and SCDAH programs have been fruitful. The state currently has 1,281 sites listed on the National Register of Historic Buildings; 152 of these sites are really districts with multiple structures, so we in fact have some 15,000 individual, recognized historic buildings scattered across the state.

Since 1966, preservation has become an area of interest to architects, for studies show that historic preservation bolsters tourism; consequently, preservation is often used as one of the tools in comprehensive economic development plans. Robert T. Lyles, AIA/SC, recently served as chairman of the Governor's Task Force on Historic Preservation and Heritage Tourism. The report by the Task Force (November 2000) noted that preservation-related construction creates more jobs than new construction, that "approximately 2.7 million heritage visitors travel to South Carolina each year," and although tourism is growing at a rate of 5% annually, heritage tourism is growing at a rate of 30%. Moreover the typical heritage tourist spends about 62% more per trip ($688) than does the average tourist.[66]

Equally important from an architect's point of view, preservation focuses on aspects of the built environment which help define a sense of place. It is not surprising that architects have taken a leading role in historic preservation in South Carolina – Albert Simons in Charleston, Walter Petty (who served on the national AIA committee to restore the Octagon in Washington, D.C.), William Fulmer and Phelps Bultman (both of whom were active in the establishment and subsequent work of

---

[65] John M. Bryan and the Triad Architectural Associates, *Preservation Case Studies: Abbeville, South Carolina* (Washington, D.C.: U.S. Department of the Interior, 1979); John M. Bryan and Riley Bultman Coulter Associates, Architects – Engineers, *Chester, S.C., A Preservation Planning Report* (Columbia: South Carolina Department of Archives and History, 1975).

[66] Governor's Task Force on Historic Preservation and Heritage Tourism, *Investing in South Carolina's Future by Preserving Our Past* (No publisher, November, 2000), 7-9.

the Columbia Landmarks Commission), Henry Boykin (especially active in the Camden area), John Califf (who directed the restoration of the South Carolina College on "the Horseshoe"), Martin Meek, who is active in restoration work in the Piedmont, and Joe Rogers (who, as a state employee within the General Services Administration, served as an architect representing the state throughout the renovation of the State House) - all of them made notable contributions.

The development of historic preservation in Charleston has been widely published, but there is no account in print of the same story in Columbia. Here, as in Charleston, AIA/SC members played leading roles.

In 1954 Columbia enacted a sub-standard housing ordinance and hired William K. Marsh as the new Housing Rehabilitation Director. Two years later Marsh hired Mrs. Mabel Payne to work in the field, and as she made inspections throughout the city she noted buildings she believed to be historic. Her lists were the foundation of the city's subsequent historic preservation programs. Mr. Marsh and Mrs. Payne established a ten member Historical Advisory Committee in 1960 in an attempt to save the Ainsley Hall House (designed by Robert Mills in 1822) and to promote "the preservation of historical homes." The threat to the Ainsley Hall house led to the formation of the Historic Columbia Foundation (1961) and the Richland County Historic Preservation Commission (1963). These groups successfully purchased, restored and opened the house to the public.

As this campaign was underway, Phillip Steadfast, City Manager, was having a zoning ordinance written for Columbia (the ordinance then in force was a copy of Atlanta's). Fred Bair, a consultant from Chicago, was drafting the new law, and he and the city manager asked local architects to help incorporate historic preservation into the new law. Walter Petty took the lead. He organized a walking tour by architects covering the two square mile original city. They took notes and photographs and mounted an exhibition in a vacant store on Main Street which created public support. As a result, provision was made in the new zoning ordinance for a Historic and Cultural Buildings Commission which was empowered to develop a list of historic buildings, delay demolition for six months and make recommendations to city council. Using maps and lists prepared by Petty, Mabel Payne and AIA/SC members, Professor Harold Cooledge of Clemson did a "windshield survey," and with only one exception, city council adopted the recommendations officially recognizing the buildings as being historic, and preservation in Columbia was underway.[67]

The AIA/SC became firmly identified with the statewide preservation effort in 1979 when it established its headquarters in a Victorian cottage on Richland Street in Columbia. William Fulmer, AIA/SC, had purchased two cottages and restored one (the Maxcy Gregg House) as professional offices. He sold the adjacent cottage to the Clemson Architectural Foundation, and the chapter, working with the CAF and the SC Department of Archives and History, created an office which had proved to be functional and – from a public relations point of view – appropriate.

Photograph by Alt Lee, Inc.

AIA/SC Cottage, Richland Street, Columbia, SC

---

[67] The beginnings of historic preservation in Columbia are based in part on a memorandum by Phelps Bultman in the Task Force files. For subsequent developments see: *LBC&W, Urban Design and Historic Preservation For Columbia* (Columbia: Central Midlands Regional Planning Council, 1974), and John M. Bryan and Associates, *City-Wide Architectural Survey and Historic Preservation Plan, Columbia, South Carolina* (Columbia: State Historic Preservation Office, 1993). The one building recommended, but not listed by city council due to objections by the owner, was an office building in the 1300 block of Main Street with an ornate terra-cotta façade. The offices of W.B. Smith Whaley had once occupied the second floor of this building.

South Carolina AIA Auxiliary

A number of architects recall that their wives made them more conscious of the relevance of historic preservation. In 1965, Othella Freeman, Elsie Wolff, Betsy Bultman, Charlotte Lewis and others initiated the creation of the Ladies Auxiliary of the SCAIA. (The name of the group was later changed to the South Carolina AIA Auxiliary.) Their objectives were to support the work of the chapter and "to stimulate interest in and knowledge of architecture, the profession of architecture and its related subjects, and to recommend and support projects which will advance the cultural arts."[68] The auxiliary first met in Florence in October 1965, and soon (1967) had 87 members. For the next 34 years they met annually. Local chapters of the auxiliary were active in Greenville (the Greenville group actually antedated the state organization and is the only chapter that is still active), Spartanburg, Columbia, Charleston, Hilton Head Island and Clemson. They all focused on raising money for architectural scholarships and historic preservation awards, promoting public educational programs and helping to plan AIA/SC meetings.[69]

Architectural Education after McClure

David Pearson served as dean of the College of Architecture 1983-1985. Upon his departure, following a national search, James F. Barker, a Clemson graduate who had been dean of the School of Architecture at Mississippi State University, became dean in 1986. To generate support for the architectural curriculum, he created a strong College Advisory Board and established a vibrant urban studies and historic preservation program in partnership with the College of Charleston. In 1989, *Architecture*, the magazine of the AIA, praised the program at Clemson as "a school in balance... where strong tradition co-exists with innovation; where campuses are both small town and urban; where faculty and students share mutual respect; where architectural education is valued, but considerate of the total development of the individual; where a strong sense of identity frees faculty and students to explore; and where student work ranges from traditional solutions to spiritual pilgrimage. Would such a school be an architectural Eden? Visit Clemson University and see." Barker's leadership, like McClure's, was soon nationally

---

[68] Othella Freeman to Betsy Bultman, July 1, 1965, a copy of a letter in the files of the History Book Task Force. Membership in the Auxiliaries dwindled in the 1980s as women entered the work force, and the statewide auxiliary formally disbanded in 1999.

[69] Lists of auxiliary officers, awards and scholarships can be found in the files of the History Book Task Force.

recognized, for in 1991 he was elected President of the Association of Collegiate Schools of Architecture.

In 1994 Clemson reorganized the administrative structure of the university into four colleges. Under the new scheme, architecture was combined with other disciplines to create the College of Architecture, Arts and Humanities, and Barker became dean of the new, larger college. José Caban, the Chair of the School of Architecture under Dean Barker, established a third off-campus program based in Barcelona, Spain. As the new millennium began, Barker, as president of the university, toured the architecture building with Dick McMahon – who had graduated from Clemson in architecture – and his wife. McMahon made an unrestricted, multimillion-dollar gift to the architecture program, a donation which will prove significant as the curriculum continues to evolve.

In 1999, Dino Curris, Clemson's president, resigned. The trustees conducted a national search, and after a stiff competition and the active support of Allen P. Wood, AIA/SC, Clemson Trustee, Barker was appointed. Barker has proved to be an energetic, active president, and as this is written he has done a stellar job in leading Clemson through the recession of 2001-2002.

Janice Schach, a landscape architect, was completing a term as President of the American Society of Landscape Architects when she became Dean of the College of Architecture, Arts and Humanities in 2000. During her first year in office, in addition to her work on campus, she has devoted time and attention to public speaking and service, continuing a tradition of outreach that began at the beginning with Pop Lee's attention to rural schools.

Fair Allocation of State Work

The need to establish a fair way to award publicly funded work was another major late 20th century issue. This problem had been confronted (unsuccessfully) by AIA/SC members in 1924. The state had authorized the expenditure of $500,000 to erect an office building adjacent the State House, and AIA/SC officers, Albert Simons, secretary treasurer, Nat Gaillard Walker, director and J.D. Newcomer, president, proposed that a competition be held, judged by a reputable outsider with contestants limited to registered architects residing in South Carolina. The commissioners appointed by the legislature listened politely, but decided to select an architect based on a series of interviews. Variations of this system continued for the following half a century.[70]

---

[70] John M. Bryan, *Creating the South Carolina State House* (Columbia: USC Press, 1999), 147.

In 1970, John W. Califf, Jr., while preparing an article for the *SCAIA Review of Architecture* "featuring some of the buildings being planned under the capital improvements bond act" found that in the recent past "for thirty-seven separate projects, totaling some $75,000,000 and involving fifteen state agencies and institutions, only nine architectural firms out of more than a hundred in the state had been selected. Of these nine firms, two had gotten more than sixty per cent of the work."

To rectify the situation, the AIA/SC board initiated discussions with state officials, and "after more than two years of committees, reports and revisions by the governor and the chapter, during which time the situation continued unabated, a new policy was adopted." In 1973, the State Budget and Control Board issued guidelines which required public notice by state agencies, the submission of qualifications, conferences with interested parties, the ranking of three qualified firms, contract negotiations, and approval or rejection of agency actions by the Budget and Control Board.[71]

The Changing Nature of Architectural Practice
Large Firms

Some of the older architects interviewed for this project lamented a tendency towards larger and larger firms and the need to consult more and more specialists. They said these trends have eroded individual, creative freedom.

We have seen, however, that large firms offering a constellation of specialized services appeared here with the textile industry in the 1880s. And as early as 1963, Henry Wright, national president of the AIA, visiting South Carolina, said "the architect's present dilemma where so many specialized disciplines are going into a building and its environment ... urged closer collaboration with the many specialized fields of design.... if the architect is to provide creative thinking, he [must] acquire a vocabulary of basic knowledge of these many technical skills.... The architect needs to broaden his knowledge beyond that of design only.... If the architect is to survive in practice, he must acquire a knowledge of business administration, economics, real estate and project financing."[72] And C.C. Wilson, discussing the profession in 1930 (as quoted above) dated the use of consultants from the widespread use of steel and reinforced concrete, that is, from the first quarter of the 20th century.

Architects have initiated and coordinated the work of other specialists for many years. It is true that the number and variety of

---

[71] "And Down in South Carolina," *SCAIA Review of Architecture* (1973), 1, 9.

[72] Interview in *Blueprint*, April 11, 1963.

specialties and sub-specialties continue to increase, but there is nothing new in the architect's role as choirmaster or conductor. Speaking directly to this point, James F. Barker, FAIA, now president of Clemson University, says "I see the architects' contributions as presenting creative and collaborative solutions.... Architects lead in collaboration... it's the very nature of what we do."[73]

Non-Traditional Employment

Another trend noted by older architects is the growing number of architects who find employment in settings beyond the traditional architectural office. Like large offices, this trend is rooted in the past. Since the early 20th century, South Carolina has benefited from the work of architect-educators, including Pop Lee, Emery Gunnin, Bob Longstreet, Joe Young, Harlan McClure and Jim Barker. Other architects have chosen to become general contractors – C.R. Dial and Albert Thomas come to mind. State government has many architects on staff, and this is not surprising, for the state owns almost 280 buildings totaling approximately 3.75 million square feet, 23,000 pieces of real estate, and a construction and maintenance budget averaging approximately $22 million dollars annually. Various state institutions and agencies are large and complex enough to employ architects. Agencies having architects include the University of South Carolina, Clemson and the Citadel, the Department of Archives and History, Vocational Rehabilitation, the Department of Transportation, Mental Health, the Department of Disabilities and Special Needs and the Office of the State Engineer. Joe Rogers, AIA, Manager of Construction and Planning for Facilities Management, an arm of the General Services Administration, observes that these architects working for agencies often serve as knowledgeable clients. Understanding their agency's needs as well as the design and construction process, enables them to define design criteria which will help the agency do its work.

Drawing and the New Technologies

Computer assisted design or drafting and digital presentation programs are often cited as important recent changes. For architects the old saying that "a picture is worth 1000 words" is an understatement. Anything that affects drawing, almost by definition, is important to the profession.

---

[73] Irene Dumas Tyson, *Architecture South Carolina* (2000), 10.

Drawings have always been the major medium used by architects to give form to ideas and then to convey the result to clients, contractors and craftsmen. Other disciplines employ specialized means of communicating data: mathematicians, physicists and chemists, for example, use formulas; cooks use recipes; musicians use a notational system. But architects' initial sketches are essentially different, for sketches are unconstrained by specific values; they are suggestive rather than prescriptive; they provide a record of the creative, imaginative beginnings of ideas which may then be manipulated rationally, ultimately

Peace Center Skyline by Dick Mitchell

Wall section by Reid Hearn

Classical Ruins by Douglas Corkern

coming to fruition as concrete, three dimensional structures in the real world. Drawings of increasing specificity often map the path from concept to completed project.

Richard Morris Hunt, the first American architect to study at the Ecole des Beaux Arts, goaded apprentices and students to make drawing a habit. Robert Swain Peabody, who worked in Hunt's office, remembered Hunt urging them to "draw, draw, draw, sketch, sketch, sketch. If you can't draw anything else, draw your boots. It will ultimately give you control of your pencil so that you can the more rightly express on paper your thoughts in designing. The greater

Cottage, Auldbrass, South Carolina
by Lynn G. Craig

Riverside Rowing Center, Columbia Canal
Kohnfirm Architecture

Poppies by Maynard Pearlstein

facility you have in expressing these thoughts, the freer and better your designs will be."[74] Hunt believed that drawing enables the architect to perceive, refine and communicate the initial, intuitive design idea. Sketches, which may appear casual, insubstantial and ill defined, often capture the kernel of an idea and provide a starting point which can be developed and refined using an array of graphic conventions and techniques.

An architect obviously needs a constellation of skills, but in this constellation, drawing is one of the brightest stars. James Barker notes "the technology of drawing and drafting ... have evolved in dramatically different ways, but the sketching line is the same .... The basic principles of eye-hand coordination and training your eye and hand to work together is a fundamental underlying principle...."[75]

The South Carolina licensing law which defines the practice of architecture implicitly recognizes that drawings are central to the profession: "Every Architect or firm practicing in this State must have a seal, the impression of which must contain the name of the Architect, his or her place of business, and the words 'Registered Architect, State of South Carolina,' with which he or she must stamp all drawings, prints and specifications for use in this State."

Technology has altered the production, reproduction and transmission of architectural drawings, but the language of drawings – the meaning and purpose served by various types of drawings – remains virtually unchanged. Since its appearance in the 1970s, CADD (computer assisted design and drawing) has proven to be a vast improvement in organizing layers of information, in assessing the implications of design alternatives, in drafting speed and accuracy. But for many architects, CADD has not replaced sketching as a form of imaginative shorthand, and many clients still respond best to a hand drawn perspective or presentation drawing, replete with evocative over-emphases and distortions. In sketches and presentation drawings we glimpse the architect's imaginative, seminal contribution to the subsequent collaboration that produces buildings.

---

[74] Catherine Howland Hunt, typescript biography of Richard Morris Hunt, Prints and Drawings Collection, The Octagon, the museum of the American Architectural Foundation, quoted by Paul R. Baker, *Richard Morris Hunt* (Cambridge: M.I.T. Press), 102.

[75] Interview, James Barker with James L. Thomas and F. Earle Gaulden, October 18, 2001.

Classical Ruins by Douglas Corkern

Honors, Awards, and Rosters of Membership

"AIA/SC has a long tradition of recognizing individuals, organizations, and projects for exemplifying the very best in architecture. The AIA believes that awards programs should be carefully structured so that selection and recognition of winners serve two distinct purposes: one directed to the profession, and the other to the public. By focusing attention on activity within the profession the general quality of architectural practice is elevated. By informing the public on the breadth and value of architectural practice, the entire profession is held in higher esteem"[76]

Honorary Members
Of the American Institute of Architects
from South Carolina

The bylaws of the American Institute of Architects provide that:

A Person of esteemed character who is not eligible for membership in the Institute but who has rendered distinguished service to the profession of architecture or the arts and sciences allied therewith may be admitted to Honorary Membership in the Institute (Chapter III, Article 3)

Honorary membership is the highest honor the American Institute of Architects can bestow upon a person outside the profession of architecture. The award is only conferred upon those whose contributions are judged to be of national significance. Nine South Carolinians have been awarded the status of Honorary AIA during the last quarter century. They are Major General Clifton D. Wright, Jr., Charles E. Fraser, Henry C. Chambers, The Honorable Joseph P. Riley, Jr., The Honorable Strom Thurmaond, M. David Egan, Roger Milliken, John M. Bryan, and The Honorable Ernest F. Hollings. They appear on the following pages with their award citations.

---

[76] Samuel B. Herin, AIA, 2001 Design Commission Chair, a memo announcing the 2001 design awards program in the Task Force files.

Major General Clifton D. Wright, Jr., Honorary AIA, 1983
Sullivans Island, South Carolina

General Wright graduated with a B. S. Degree in Architectural Engineering from the College of Architecture at Clemson University and later a Master's Degree in Management from the George Washington University. He has maintained a keen interest in architecture since being commissioned a 2nd Lieutenant in the United States Air Force in 1955. General Wright has been able to affect substantial change and improvement in the built environment during his 27 years of service in architecture, engineering, and construction divisions of the Air Force. During his distinguished military career he has constantly been an advocate of both architectural professionalism and architectural design quality.

Throughout all of his prestigious assignments, General Wright strengthened programs that fostered design quality in architecture, landscape architecture and interior design. As Director of Engineering and Services Headquarters, U.S. Air Force, he had worldwide influence on design and construction excellence.

He developed an Air Force architectural internship program that was acceptable to the American Institute of Architects. He also instituted Air Force Design Awards programs, schools to familiarize Air Force personnel with programming in design disciplines, and symposiums centered on improving design quality at Air Force installations.

Charles E. Fraser, Honorary AIA, 1983
Hilton Head Island, South Carolina

Mr. Fraser's success as a developer of planned communities with unusual vision is acknowledged worldwide. His perception and talent for bringing together the best in professional expertise and giving leadership in planning projects transforming tranquil, undisturbed woodlands into delightful, livable communities extends beyond the usual bounds.

On Hilton Head Island, South Carolina, his projects of Sea Pines Plantation and Harbour Town exemplify the best aspects of design in which the built and natural environments are harmoniously combined.

In 1968, the national AIA recognized Mr. Fraser with a "Citation for Excellence in Private Community Planning," the first U.S. recipient of the award.

**Henry C. Chambers,
Honorary AIA, 1986
Beaufort, South Carolina**

As a resident and mayor of the City of Beaufort, Henry C. Chamber initiated and directed the revitalization of this historic community and the re-development of its waterfront. His vision has encompassed all aspects of the cityscape from the creation of a master plan, the production of a practical preservation manual, signage and economic development. Mr. Chambers has made it possible for architectural students to play a constructive role in many of his projects; he is a trustee of the Clemson Advancement Foundation and a consistent financial supporter of its work.

**The Honorable Joseph P. Riley, Jr.,
Honorary AIA, 1987
Charleston, South Carolina**

Mayor Riley, through his leadership and clear vision of Charleston as a continuum of excellence in architecture, has rendered outstanding service to our profession that is of historical significance. Mayor Riley has demonstrated a strong conviction of incorporating beauty into new projects while preserving the city's distinctive and rich architectural heritage. Evidence of this conviction can be seen in the redevelopment of housing in Charleston's poorer sections, the Cooper River waterfront park, Charleston Place – a world-class convention center in the heart of the historic cityscape, the Visitors' Center, the Aquarium;

these, and numerous other project throughout the city attest to Mayor Riley's vision, energy, and perseverance.

During his tenure, Mayor Riley has been the recipient of many awards for his leadership in preserving Charleston's rich architectural heritage. As a leader in the United States Conference of Mayors, he has demonstrated the value of architectural consciousness to mayors across the country.

**The Honorable Strom Thurmond,
Honorary AIA, 1990
United States Senate**

The many facets of public life which have made Senator Strom Thurmond a legend are joined by his outstanding service to our profession in historically significant initiatives. His commitment to the preservation of important structures has benefited the nation. He has been a steadfast supporter of the National Register of Historic Places. In the 101st Congress, Senator Thurmond co-sponsored legislation to establish a federal trust fund for historic preservation, the American Heritage Trust Act. He was the chief sponsor of the bill to construct a memorial to the veterans of World War II in the nation's capital. Senator Thurmond was an active member of the American Commission on the Bicentennial, Washington, DC, which has worked to preserve the sites of important events relating to the U.S. Constitution and the Declaration of Independence.

By donating his papers to the Strom Thurmond Institute at Clemson University, Senator Thurmond was instrumental in the creation of this six million dollar government and public policy center.

**M. David Egan,
Honorary AIA, 1991**

M. David Egan has spent his professional career promoting a better understanding of the crucial relationship between design theory and the technical theory of acoustics, lighting, fire safety, and mechanical systems. With his lectures and seminars given throughout the United States and as far away as Singapore and Saudia Arabia, he has motivated hundreds of students and professionals to achieve design excellence by integrating acoustics, lighting, and mechanical systems in their designs. His books on these subjects are used at most schools of architecture, and he has served as the consultant-of-record on hundreds of projects ranging over a wide variety of building types. He is an effective speaker and is well known and accepted as an expert in both the educational and professional realms.

In 1990 Professor Egan was awarded the "Certificate of Excellence" for National AIA Education Honors for his significant contributions to architectural education and to the profession of architecture.

**Roger Milliken,
Honorary AIA, 1992
Spartanburg, South Carolina**

Roger Milliken is the chairman and CEO of the world's largest privately owned textile company. His vision, enthusiasm, knowledge and energy during more than sixty years has inspired excellence in architecture and landscape design. Milliken facilities are synonymous with design excellence.

Mr. Milliken's vision and energy are felt beyond his own company through his service on institutional and civic boards. Wofford College, Converse College and the Greenville-Spartanburg Airport are examples of institutions beyond his own corporate facilities that have benefited from his support and architectural sensitivity.

**John M. Bryan,
Honorary AIA, 1995
The University of South Carolina**

Professor Bryan teaches art and architectural history at the University of South Carolina. He has organized two national exhibitions for the AIA, one devoted to the drawings of Robert Mills and the other celebrating the centennial of Biltmore Estate. Professor Bryan has published books, articles and encyclopedia entries in France, England and the United States. He has worked as an architectural historian and historic preservation planner and has received the Order of the Palmetto from the State of South Carolina, a national book award from the American Victorian Society, a national Medal of Honor from the Daughters of the American Revolution, an award for Research in the Humanities from the University of South Carolina Educational Foundation and a Medal of Distinction for Contributions to the Profession from the AIA/SC.

**The Honorable Ernest F. Hollings,
Honorary AIA
United States Senate**

Throughout his career, Fritz Hollings has been an effective advocate for historic preservation. As an attorney, he restored the Farmers and Exchange Bank (East Bay Street, Charleston) as a law office. As junior senator from South Carolina, he has supported our architectural heritage in a number of ways. His efforts were pivotal in the campaign to save Snee Farm. He was instrumental in saving Tibwin Plantation which was acquired by the U. S. Forest Service. He backed legislation which has facilitated the restoration of historic black colleges and universities across the country, and his support has been crucial in the preservation of South Carolina's historic Penn center.

Honorary Affiliate Members
South Carolina Chapter
American Institute of Architects

Honorary affiliate is a membership classification for individuals who are not architects and have made significant contributions to the profession.

Kenneth A. Bingham
Representative, SC General Assembly

Henry Cato
Representative, SC General Assembly

Henry Chambers
Beaufort Realty

James E. Clyburn
U.S. Congressman

Robert D. Coble
Mayor, City of Columbia

M. David Egan
Professor Emeritus,
Construciton Science and Management
Clemson University

Barbara Harper
Former Executive Director,
SC Board of Architectural Examiners

Robert W. Harrell, Jr.
Representative, SC General Assembly

Hugh K. Leatherman, Sr.
Senator, SC Genreral Assembly

Phil P. Leventis
Senator, SC General Assembly

Glenn F. McConnell
Senator, SC General Assemblly

Robert E. McNair
Former Governor of South Carolina

Richard W. Riley
Former Governor of South Carolina
Former U.S. Secretary of Education

Mark Sanford
Governor of South Carolina

Janice Schach, FASLA
Dean, College of Architecture, Arts
  and Humanities,
Clemson University

James E. Smith, Jr.
Representative, SC General Assembly

Verne Smith
Senator, SC General Assembly

Inez Moore Tenenbaum
SC Superintendent of Education

Clifton Duke Wright
Retired Air Force Major General

Medal of Distinction Recipients
South Carolina Chapter
American Institute of Architects

The Medal of Distinction is the highest honor that AIA/SC can bestow upon a AIA/SC member. The State AIA Board of Directors confers it in recognition of a significant body of work and/or service that has made a lasting influence on the practice of architecture in South Carolina.

James C. Hemphill, AIA
Distinguished Service Award, 1966

Harlan E. McClure, FAIA
Dean Emeritus,
College of Architecture,
Clemson University
Medal of Distinction, 1993

F. Earle Gaulden, FAIA
Craig, Gaulden & Davis, Inc.
Medal of Distinction, 1995

Frank E. Lucas, FAIA
LS3P Associates, Ltd.
Medal of Distinction, 1997

James A. Neal, FAIA
Neal-Prince & Partners, Inc.
Medal of Distinction, 1999

Kirk R. Craig, FAIA
Craig, Gaulden & Davis, Inc.
Medal of Distinction, 2001

Firm Awards
South Carolina Chapter
American Institute of Architects

The Firm Award is the highest honor that AIA/SC can bestow upon a South Carolina architectural firm. The AIA/SC Board of Directors confers it in recognition of a significant body of work and/or service that has made a lasting influence on the practice of architecture in South Carolina.

Craig, Gaulden & Davis, 1993
Greenville, SC

LS3P Associates, Ltd., 1995
Charleston, SC

Neal-Prince & Partners, 1997
Greenville, SC

Stevens & Wilkinson of SC, Inc., 2001
Columbia, SC

Alliance Award Recipients
South Carolina Chapter
American Institute of Architects

The Alliance Award recognizes allied professionals (contractors, engineers, landscape architects, interior designers, etc.) that have consistently demonstrated the spirit of strategic cooperation and contributions to the profession. This award can be given in three categories: Non-architect, Architectural Reporting and Government Affairs.

John Bryan, 1995
University of South Carolina

John Kent, 1995
Office of School Facilities

***Post & Courier*, 1995**
Charleston, SC

Lewis & Clark, Craftsmen
Columbia, SC

Robert Behre, 2001
Post & Courier

Doug Harper, 2001
Harper Corporation, General Contractors

Design Awards
The American Institute of Architects

The national AIA awards committee recognizes exemplary projects and designs deemed nationally significant.

The University of South Carolina Undergraduate Library, LBC&W and Edward D. Stone, First Honor Award, 1963

Middleton Inn, Charleston, Clarke and Menefee, Honor Award, 1987

Reid House, Charleston, Clarke and Menefee, Architects, Honor Award, 1990

Charleston Cottages, Charleston, Chris Schmitt & Associates, Christopher Rose, Design Architect, Honor Award, 1991

Middleton Inn, Charleston,
Clarke and Menefee,

Photograph by R. Christian Schmitt

Charleston Cottages, Charleston,
Chris Schmitt & Associates

Design Awards
South Atlantic Region
The American Institute of Architects

The South Atlantic Region of the AIA recognizes the outstanding work of its members.

Undergraduate Library, University of South Carolina, LBC&W and Edward D. Stone, Honor Award, 1959

Architect's Residence, William Speer, AIA, Honor Award, 1959

City Parking Garage, Columbia, LBC&W, Merit Award, 1966

Turtle Lane Cabanas, Corkern, Wiggins & Associates, Honor Award, 1966

Regional Postal Distribution Center Prototype, Florence, LBC&W, Honor Award, 1976

Henry C. Chambers Park, Beaufort, Thomas & Denzinger, Honor Award, 1982

John A. Sibler Horticulture Center, Pine Mountain, Georgia, Craig, Gaulden & Davis and Robert E. Marvin, Honor Award, 1984

Harbor Observation Tower, Port Royal, Thomas & Denzinger Architects, 1990

Charleston Cottages, Chris Schmitt & Associates, Inc., Christopher Rose Design Architect, Merit Award, 1992

Mill Entrance and Visitors' Orientation Center, Union Camp Corp., Eastover, CRSS Architects, Inc., Honor Award, 1992

188 St. Philip Street Apartments, Charleston, Schmitt, Sampson Walker, Honor Award, 2000

Saks Fifth Avenue Majestic Square, Charleston, LS3P Associates, Ltd., Merit Award, 2000

The South Carolina State House Renovation, Columbia, Stevens & Wilkinson of SC, Inc., Merit Award, 2000

Tamassee-Salem Middle/High School, Salem, LS3P Associates, Ltd., Merit Award, 2000

© 2001 Gary Knight + Associates, Inc.

South Carolina State House Renovation, Columbia, Stevens & Wilkinson of SC, Inc.

© 2001 Gary Knight + Associates, Inc.

© Rick Alexander and Associates, Inc.

Saks Fifth Avenue Majestic Square, Charleston, LS3P Associates, Ltd.

111

Design Awards
South Carolina Chapter
The American Institute of Architects

As with the South Atlantic Region, the AIA/SC Design Awards are selected from projects submitted by architects by juries made up of non-resident professionals, usually architects. Juries, at their discretion, determine numbers and designations of awards.

Elmwood Cemetery Bell Tower, LBC&W, First Honor, 1962

Science Building, North, Greenville Jr. College, Lillard, Westmoreland, McGarity, Honor Award, 1962

Women's Residence Hall, Clemson, Hallman & Weems, Honor Award, 1964

Forest Lake Country Club, Columbia, LBC&W, Honor Award, 1964

Crosrol Carding Dev. Inc., Greenville, Craig & Gaulden, Honor Award, 1966

Dr. and Mrs. Marion G. Vanfossen's Residence, Greenville, Craig & Gaulden, Design Citation, 1966

Rutledge Office Building, LBC&W, Design Award, 1966

Women's Dormitory, University of South Carolina, LBC&W, Design Citation, 1966

Robert Muldrow Cooper Library, Clemson, LBC&W, 1st Honor Award, 1967

Bordeleau Apartment, Charleston, Lucus & Stubbs, Commendation, 1967

U.S. Post Office, Columbia, LBC&W and Lafaye, Fair, Lafaye Associates, Honor Award, 1968

Oak-Read Apartments, Columbia, LBC&W, Merit Award, 1968

Humanities Center, University of South Carolina, LBC&W, Honor Award,

1970
Carolina Coliseum, LBC&W, Honor Award, 1970

News Piedmont Office, Greenville, J.E. Sirrine Company, Merit Award, 1970

Littlejohn Coliseum, Clemson, J.E. Sirrine Company, Merit Award, 1970

Auditorium/Exhibition Hall, Lucas & Stubbs, Merit Award, 1970

Bates House, University of South Carolina, Maynard Pearlstine and Upshur, Riley & Bultman, Merit Award, 1970

Bates House, University of South Carolina, Maynard Pearlstine and Upshur, Riley & Bultman

Photograph by Russell Maxey

WNOK TV-Radio Studio and Offices, Columbia, Maynard Pearlstine and William Fulmer, Merit Award, 1970

Mental Health Center, Greenville, Harold Mack & Associates, Merit Award, 1970

Science Wing Addition, Dreher High School, Columbia, Upshur, Riley, and Bultman, Merit Award, 1970

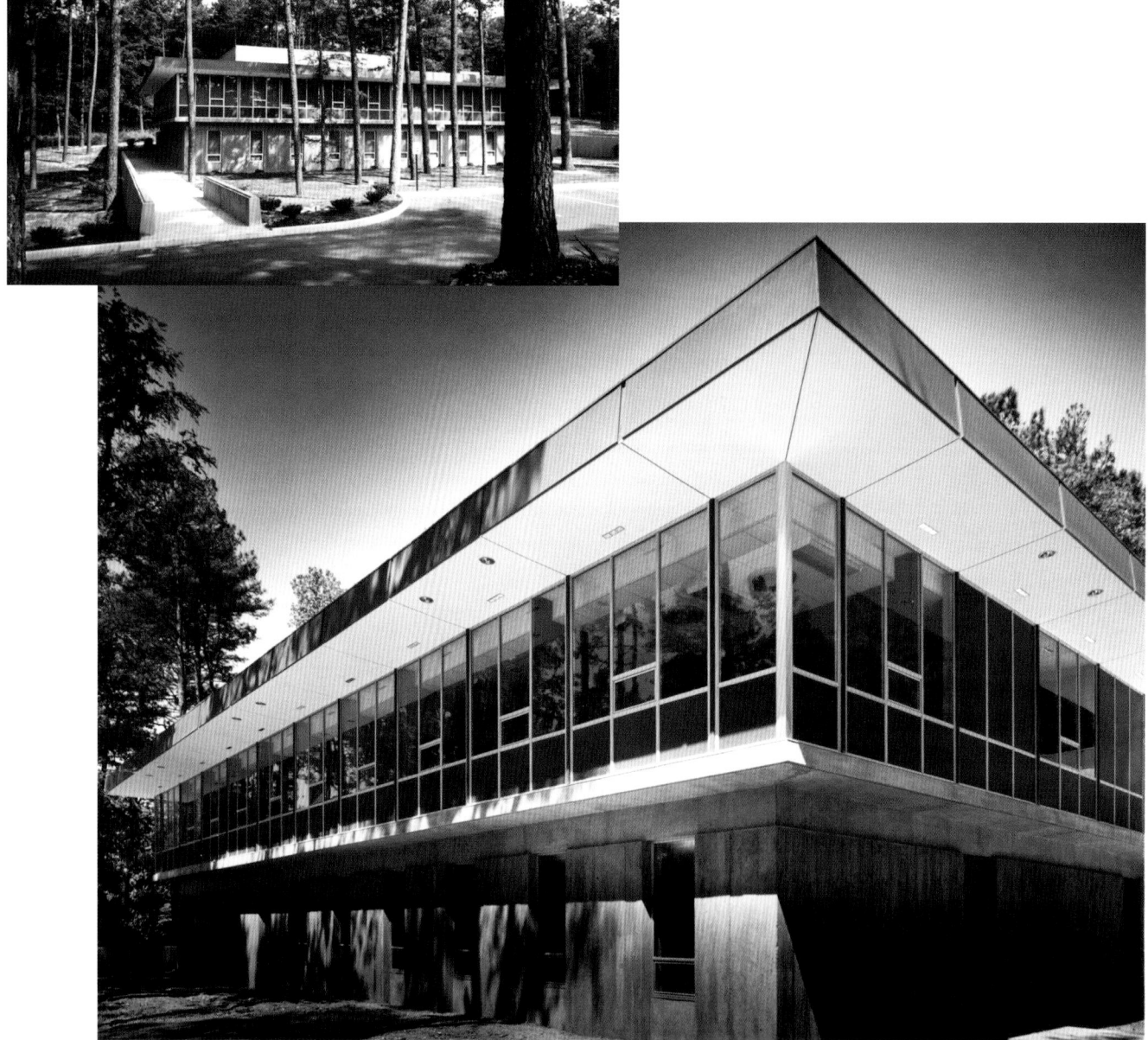

Photographs by Russell Maxey

WNOK TV-Radio Studio and Offices, Columbia,
Maynard Pearlstine and William Fulmer

J. Drake Edens Library, Columbia College, Upshur, Riley and Bultman, Merit Award, 1970

Orangeburg-Calhoun Technical College, LBC&W, Merit Award, 1970

Library, Wofford College, LBC&W, Merit Award, 1970

Shipyard Condominium, Hilton Head Island, McGinty & Dye, Honor Award, 1972

Our Shepherd Lutheran Church, Hartsville, Tarleton-Tankersley, Honor Award, 1972

Sadler's Creek Bath House-Pavilion, Lake Hartwell, J.E. Sirrine, Honor Award, 1972

Six Patio Homes, Hilton Head Island, Columbia Architectural Group, Honor Award, 1974

Hollis and Hawkins Law Offices, Charleston, Lucas & Stubbs, Honor Award, 1974

Photograph by Russell Maxey

Science Wing Addition, Dreher High School, Columbia, Upshur, Riley, and Bultman

Pavilion & Bath House, Baker Creek State Park, Pearlstine/Anderson, Honor Award, 1974

College of Business Administration, University of South Carolina, Gieger, McElveen and Kennedy and Curtis & Davis, Merit Award, 1974

Ingemar Falkehog Residence, Mount Pleasant, Getraude Dilling, Merit Award, 1974

Raintree Apartments, Columbia, Columbia Architectural Group, Merit Award, 1974

Cherokee County Library, Gaffney, Craig & Gaulden, Merit Award, 1974

Springs Mills Research & Development Building, Fort Mill, J.E. Sirrine, Merit Award, 1974

First Federal Savings & Loan Association Branch Office, Easley, Freeman, Wells and Major, Merit Award, 1974

Regional Postal Distribution Center Prototype, Florence, LBC&W, Honor Award, 1976

Moss Creek Plantation Club House, Hilton Head Island, Corkern & Associates, Honor Award, 1976

An Architectural Office, Greenville, Craig & Gaulden, Honor Award, 1976

Sparrow Pond Cottages, Kiawah Island, Myles Glick, Honor Award, 1978

First Federal Savings, Greenville, Freeman, Wells and Major, Honor Award, 1978

Museum of Art, Greenville, Craig & Gaulden, Honor Award, 1978

Deas Hall, The Citadel, Lucas & Stubbs, Merit Award, 1978

Police Station, Clemson, Synergy and Peter Lee, Merit Award, 1978

University Square, Clemson, Freeman, Wells and Major, Merit Award, 1978

Pavilion & Bath House, Baker Creek State Park,
Pearlstine/Anderson

College of Business Administration, University of South Carolina,
Gieger, McElveen and Kennedy and Curtis & Davis

Student Housing, Lander College, Neal Associates, Merit Award, 1978

Perone Residence, Greenville, Neal Associates, Honorable Mention, 1978

Golf Pro Shop, Hilton Head Island, James P. Brown, Honorable Mention, 1978

Doubleday Plant, Orange, Virginia, Daniel International, Honorable Mention, 1978

The Penney House, Thompson E. Penney, Honor Award, 1980

Garden Theater, Rosenblum & Associates, Honor Award, 1980

G. Werber Bryan Psychiatric Hospital, Columbia, Tarleton & Tankersley Architectural Group, Merit Award, 1980

Salt Marsh Cottages, Hilton Head Island, Lee & Partners, Merit Award, 1980

East Bay Community Center, Charleston, Lucas & Stubbs, Merit Award, 1980

The Albert Simons Center for the Arts, Charleston, Lucas & Stubbs, Merit Award, 1980

© Gordon Schenck

The Penney House,
Thompson E. Penney

Dorchester County Library, St. George, Lucas & Stubbs, Merit Award, 1980

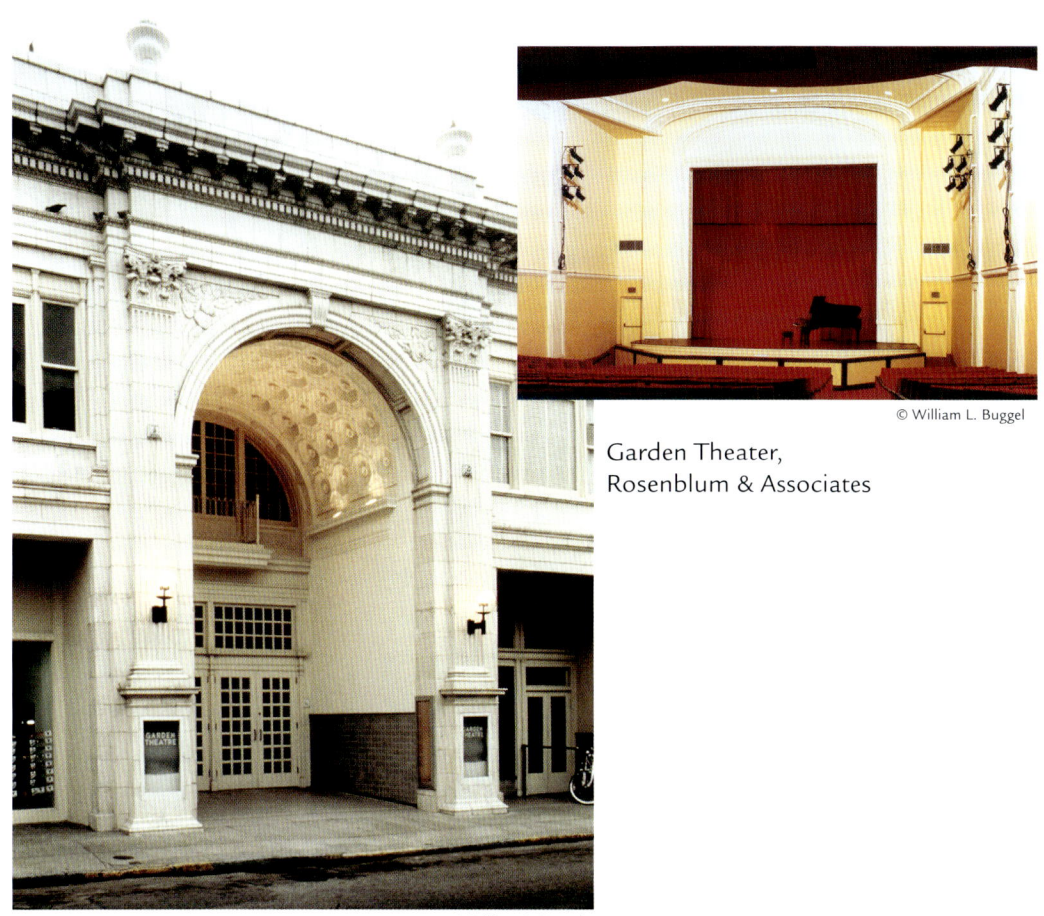

© William L. Buggel

Garden Theater,
Rosenblum & Associates

© William L. Buggel

© Gordon Schenck

Dorchester County Library, St. George,
Lucas & Stubbs

119

Richland County Judicial Center, Columbia, Geiger/McElveen/Kennedy, Honor Award, 1982

Turnberry Village Condominiums, Lee & Partners, Honor Award, 1982

Sirrine Office Building, Research Triangle, NC, J.E. Sirrine Co., Honor Award, 1982

Witherspoon Residence, Clemson, Witherspoon/Knowland, Merit Award, 1982

The Palmer Residence, Randall Inabinet, Merit Award, 1982

Richland County Judicial Center, Columbia, Geiger/McElveen/Kennedy

Savings and Loan Branch, Charleston, Lucas & Stubbs, Merit Award, 1982

Elliot House, Charleston, David J. Shaw, Special Award, 1982

Ronald McDonald House, Charleston, LS3P, Honor Award, 1984

© 1985 William Cornelia

Turnberry Village Condominiums,
Lee & Partners

© Rick Alexander and Associates, Inc.

Ronald McDonald House, Charleston,
LS3P

Forestry Research Addition to the Hutter House, LS3P, Honor Award, 1984

York County Library, York, Craig, Gaulden, and Davis, Merit Award, 1984

S.C. Public Service Authority, LS3P, Merit Award, 1984

University of South Carolina Horseshoe Restoration and Adaptive Use, John Califf, Merit Award, 1984

International Longshoremen's Association Local 1422, Charleston, Ray Huff Architects, P.A., Honor Award, 1986

Gibbes Green, University of South Carolina, Stevens & Wilkinson, Honor Award, 1986

Photograph by Russell Maxey

University of South Carolina Horseshoe Restoration and Adaptive Use, John Califf

International Longshoremen's Association Local 1422, Charleston,
Ray Huff Architects, P.A.

© Rick Alexander and Associates, Inc.

First Citizens Bank Building, Charleston, Glick/Schmitt & Associates, Honor Award, 1986

Firehouse Sixteen, Charleston, LS3P, Honor Award, 1986

John A. Sibley Horticultural Center, Pine Mountain, Georgia, Craig, Gaulden and Davis, Honor Award, 1986

Westvaco Forest Science Laboratory, Summerville, LS3P, Honor Award, 1986

First Citizens Bank Building, Charleston, Glick/Schmitt & Associates

Westvaco Forest Science Laboratory, Summerville,
LS3P

Reston Visitors' Center, Reston, Virginia, Doug Corkern Architects, Merit Award, 1986

Windmill Harbour Sportscenter, Hilton Head Island, Archipelagos, Merit Award, 1986

Recreation Building, Goodale State Park, Kershaw County, Paul Pushkar, Merit Award, 1986

Lady's Island Middle School, Beaufort, Thomas & Denzinger Architects, Merit Award, 1986

Dataw Gold Clubhouse, Dataw Island, Doug Corkern Architects, Merit Award 1986

California Dreaming Restaurant, Columbia, Stevens & Wilkinson, Merit Award, 1986

Tri-County Technical College Laboratory Classroom Facility, F.J. Clark, Honor Award, 1988

© Rick Alexander and Associates, Inc.

Tri-County Technical College Laboratory Classroom Facility, F.J. Clark

© Rick Alexander and Associates, Inc.

Receptee Barracks with Dining Facility, Fort Benning, Georgia, LS3P, Honor Award, 1988

St. Francis of Assisi Episcopal Church, Boudreaux, Hultstrand & Carter, Honor Award, 1988

Photograph by P. Douglas Quackenbush, AIA

St. Francis of Assisi Episcopal Church, Boudreaux, Hultstrand & Carter

King's Bay Enlisted Dining Facility, King's Bay, Georgia, LS3P, Honor Award, 1988

Richland School District Two Administration Building, Boudreaux, Hultstrand & Carter, Merit Award, 1988

McEntire Fire Station, McEntire Air Base, Greene & Associates, Merit Award, 1988

Renovations to the South Caroliniana Library, Drafts & Jumper Architects, Merit Award, 1988

King's Bay Enlisted Dining Facility, King's Bay, Georgia, LS3P

Columbia Bible College Prayer Chapel, Columbia, Boudreaux, Hultstrand & Carter, Merit Award, 1988

29 East Battery Renovation, Charleston, Rosenblum & Associates, Merit Award, 1988

© 1991 Rion Rizzo/Creative Sources Photography, Inc.

Columbia Bible College Prayer Chapel, Columbia,
Boudreaux, Hultstrand & Carter

Commissioners of Public Works, Charleston, LS3P, Merit Award, 1988

Harbor Observation Tower, Port Royal, Thomas and Denzinger Architects, Honor Award, 1990

Seaside at Wild Dunes, Isle of Palms, Chris Schmitt & Associates, Inc., Honor Award, 1990

Addition to First Presbyterian Church, Greenville, Craig, Gaulden & Davis, Honor Award, 1990

The Single House, Georgetown, Steven Goggans & Associates, Honor Award, 1990

Koger Center for the Arts, University of South Carolina, Geiger/McElveen/Kennedy, Honor Award, 1990

© Gordon Schenck

Commissioners of Public Works, Charleston,
LS3P

Koger Center for the Arts, University of South Carolina,
Geiger/McElveen/Kennedy

Brays Island Plantation, Sheldon, Chris Schmitt and Associates, Honor Award, 1990

Mill Entrance and Visitors' Orientation Center, Union Camp Corp., Eastover, CRSS Architects, Inc., Honor Award, 1992

Lexington State Bank Greyhound Bus Depot Renovation, Columbia, Michael Kohn and Jumper, Stewart, Carter, Sease Architects, Honor Award, 1992

First Union Center, Charleston, LS3P, Honor Award, 1992

Van Bueren Residence, Brays Island Plantation, Beaufort County, Thomas & Denzinger, Honor Award, 1992

John's Island Post Office, John's Island, Thomas & Denzinger, Honor Award, 1992

Bray's Island Gun Club, Beaufort County, Thomas & Denzinger, Honor Award, 1992

St. Peter's Regional Education Center, Columbia, Boudreaux, Hultstrand & Carter, Honor Award, 1994

© Rick Alexander and Associates, Inc.

Lexington State Bank Greyhound Bus Depot Renovation, Columbia, Michael Kohn and Jumper, Stewart, Carter, Sease Architects

© Rick Alexander and Associates, Inc.

First Union Center, Charleston,
LS3P

© 1993 Rion Rizzo/Creative Sources Photography, Inc.

St. Peter's Regional Education Center, Columbia,
Boudreaux, Hultstrand & Carter

Pivate Residence, Brays Island, Sheldon, Chris Schmitt & Associates, Honor Award, 1994

Residence at 3 Gibbes Street, Charleston, Glick/Boehm & Associates, Merit Award, 1994

Charleston Visitors Reception and Transportation Center, Charleston, Cooper, Robertson & Partners and Goff-D'Antonio, Merit Award, 1994

Socastee United Methodist Church, Myrtle Beach, S. Derrick Mozingo Associates, Merit Award, 1994

Arizona Bar & Grill, Charleston, Chris Schmitt & Associates, Merit Award, 1994

Shuler Veterinary Clinic, Mount Pleasant, Stubbs Muldrow Herin Architects, Merit Award, 1994

Riverbanks Zoo Farm, Columbia, LS3P, Merit Award, 1996

Providence Presbyterian Church, Hilton Head Island, The FWA Group, Merit Award, 1996

Shanklin Elementary School, Beaufort, Thomas & Denzinger, Merit Award, 1996

Charleston Garden, Charleston, Chris Schmitt & Associates, Merit Award, 1996

Education Center, Ravenel, LS3P, Merit Award, 1996

Bus Stop Shelter, Mount Pleasant, Stubbs Muldrow Herin Architects, Merit Award, 1996

Visitors' Center, Brookgreen Gardens, Craig, Gaulden & Davis, Energy Award, 1996

The South Carolina Model, Charleston, Chris Schmitt & Associates, Certificate Award, 1996

Affordable Efficiency Apartment, Charleston, Chris Schmitt & Associates, Certificate, 1996

Estill Federal Correction Institute, Estill, LS3P, Certificate, 1996

A Beach House, Sullivan's Island, Ray Huff Architects, P.A., Honor Award, 1997

© 2003 Starling Productions/Orlando

A Beach House, Sullivan's Island,
Ray Huff Architects

Conference Center Facility, Calhoun County, Ray Huff Architects, P.A., Merit Award, 1997

Richland County Public Library, Columbia, Stevens & Wilkinson of SC, Citation Award, 1997

Richland County Public Library, Columbia,
Stevens & Wilkinson of SC

Charleston County Health Complex Parking Garage, Charleston, LS3P,
Citation, 1997

Rhett's Bluff Landing, Kiawah Island, Schmitt Sampson Architects,
Citation, 1997

School of Music, University of South Carolina, Craig, Gaulden & Davis,
Citation, 1997

© Rion Rizzo/Creative Sources Photography, Inc.

Rhett's Bluff Landing, Kiawah Island,
Schmitt Sampson Architects

© 1995 Brian Dressler

School of Music, University of South Carolina,
Craig, Gaulden & Davis

Episcopal Church of the Holy Comforter Addition, Sumter, Boykin & Munnerlyn Architects & Associates, Citation, 1997

Roper Hospital Interdenominational Chapel, Charleston, LS3P, Associate, Citation, 1997

McDowell Residence, Spring Island, Schmitt Sampson Architects, Honor Award, 1998

Photograph by Henry D. Boykin

Episcopal Church of the Holy Comforter Addition, Sumter,
Boykin & Munnerlyn Architects & Associates

McDowell Residence, Spring Island,
Schmitt Sampson Architects

Piedmont Wilderness Institute, Laurens, Neal-Prince & Partner, Honor Award, 1998

Southend Brewery & Smokehouse, Charleston, LS3P Associates, Honor Award, 1998

Robert A. Kennedy Memorial Library, Drayton Hall Plantation, Charleston, Thomas & Denzinger Architects, Honor Award, 1998

Gordon H. Garrett Academy of Technology, Charleston, Rosenblum & Associates, Merit Award, 1998

Combat Training Pool, Marine Corps Recruit Depot, Parris Island, Thomas & Denzinger Architects, Merit Award, 1998

© Rick Alexander and Associates, Inc.

Southend Brewery & Smokehouse, Charleston,
LS3P Associates

University of South Carolina Athletic Practice Facility, Columbia, The Boudreaux Group, Honor Award, 1999

Tomasee-Salem Middle/High School Addition, Salem, LS3P, Honor Award, 1999

© 1997 Rion Rizzo/Creative Sources Photography, Inc.

University of South Carolina Athletic Practice Facility, Columbia, The Boudreaux Group

Newberry Opera House Historic Restoration, Newberry, Craig, Gaulden & Davis, Merit Award, 1999

SCDHR Composite Office Facility, Charleston, Liollio Architecture, Merit Award, 1999

Pawleys Island Post Office, Pawleys Island, Glick/Boehm & Associates, Citation, 1999

Taft/Paulsen Residence, Kiawah Island, Thomas & Denzinger Architects, Citation Awards, 1999

© 1998 Rion Rizzo/Creative Sources Photography, Inc.

Newberry Opera House Historic Restoration, Newberry,
Craig, Gaulden & Davis

SCDHR Composite Office Facility, Charleston,
Liollio Architecture

Pawleys Island Post Office, Pawleys Island,
Glick/Boehm & Associates

Whitehall Plantation, Stables, Green Pond, Schmitt Sampson Walker Architects, Honor Award, 2001

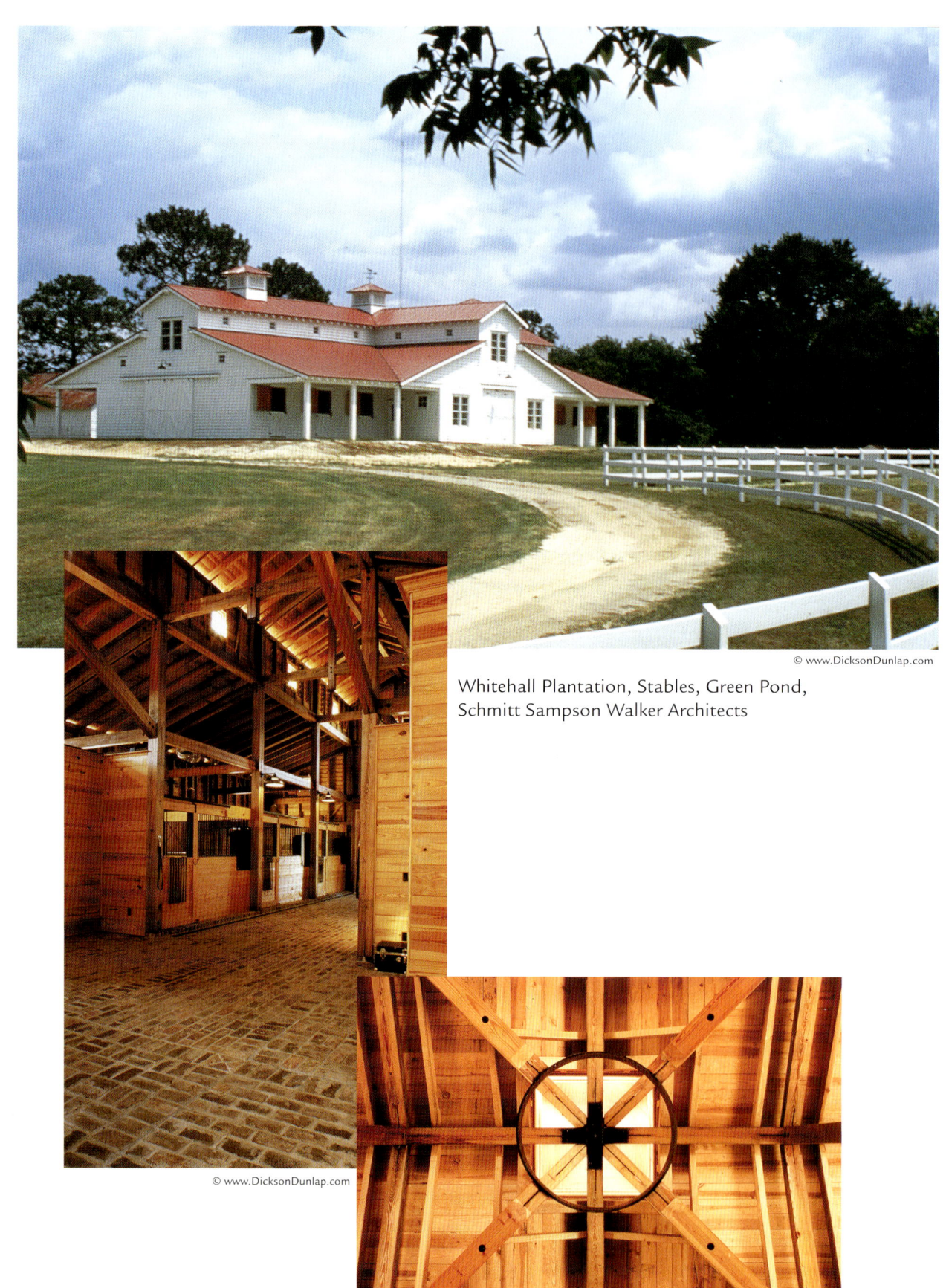

Whitehall Plantation, Stables, Green Pond,
Schmitt Sampson Walker Architects

Logan Elementary School Renovation, Addition, Columbia, The Boudreaux Group, Honor Award, 2001

© 2000 Rion Rizzo/Creative Sources Photography, Inc.

© 2000 Rion Rizzo/Creative Sources Photography, Inc.

© 2000 Rion Rizzo/Creative Sources Photography, Inc.

Logan Elementary School Renovation, Addition, Columbia, The Boudreaux Group

The S. C. State House Historic Renovation, Columbia, Stevens & Wilkinson, Merit Award, 2001

A Private Residence, Bray's Island, Thomas & Denzinger, Merit Award, 2001

Marguerite H. Brown Municipal Center, Goose Creek, Thomas & Denzinger, Merit Award, 2001

A Private Residence, Bray's Island, Thomas & Denzinger

© William Struhs

Marguerite H. Brown Municipal Center, Goose Creek, Thomas & Denzinger

Photographs by Hermann Denzinger

Photographs by Hermann Denzinger

Office of Watson Tate Savory, Columbia, Watson Tate Savory, Honor Award, 2002

Office of Watson Tate Savory, Columbia,
Watson Tate Savory

St. Mary Help of Christians - Additions, Aiken, The Boudreaux Group, Merit Award, 2002

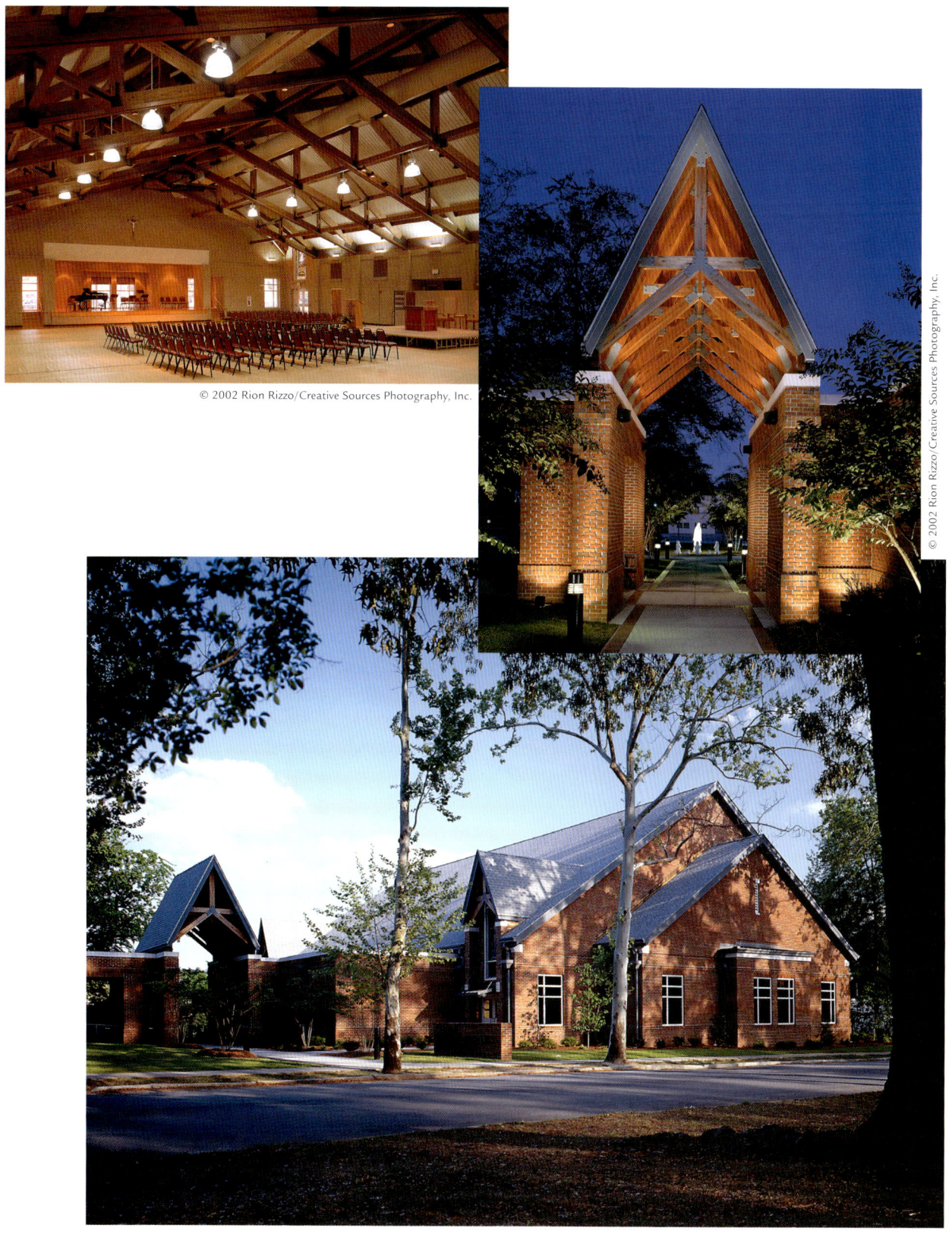

St. Mary Help of Christians - Additions, Aiken,
The Boudreaux Group

Charleston Air Force Base Chapel, Charleston, Glick/Boehm & Associates, Inc., Merit Award, 2002

© 1991 Rion Rizzo/Creative Sources Photography, Inc.

Charleston Air Force Base Chapel, Charleston, Glick/Boehm & Associates, Inc.

© 1991 Rion Rizzo/Creative Sources Photography, Inc.

The Golf Houses at Spring Island, Spring Island, Thomas & Denzinger, Architects, Merit Award, 2002

Old Beaufort College Building, Beaufort, Liollio Architecture, Merit Award, 2002

The Golf Houses at Spring Island, Spring Island,
Thomas & Denzinger

Old Beaufort College Building, Beaufort,
Liollio Architecture

A Residence, Kiawah Island, Thomas & Denzinger, Architects, Merit Award, 2002

Saks Fifth Avenue Majestic Square, Charleston, LS3P Architects, Merit Award, 2002

A Residence, Kiawah Island,
Thomas & Denzinger, Architects

Saks Fifth Avenue Majestic Square, Charleston, LS3P Architects

Robert Mills Residential Design Awards

Colt Guest House, Spring Island, Schmitt Sampson Walker, Inc., Honor Award, 2002

Rothnie Residence, Brays Island, Schmitt Sampson Walker, Inc., Honor Award, 2002

Showcase Home for Brookgreen Gardens, Murrells Inlet, Steve Goggans & Associates, Inc., Merit Award, 2002

Garonzik Residence, Schmitt Sampson Walker, Inc., Spring Island, Honor Award, 2002

The Hibben House, Mount Pleasant, Stubbs, Muldrow, Herin, Architects, Inc., Honor Award, 2002

Cornwell-Walker Residence, Greenville, Craig, Gaulden & Davis, Inc., Honor Award, 2002

The Magna Residence, Kiawah Island, Thomas & Denzinger, Architects, Honor Award, 2002

The Ackerman Residence, Brays Island, Frederick & Frederick, Architects, Honor Award, 2002

Stuart Residence, Kiawah Island, Christopher Rose, Architects, Merit Award

Colt Guest House, Spring Island,
Schmitt Sampson Walker, Inc.

Rothnie Residence, Brays Island,
Schmitt Sampson Walker, Inc.

Garonzik Residence,
Schmitt Sampson Walker, Inc.

Cornwell-Walker Residence, Greenville,
Craig, Gaulden & Davis, Inc.

The Magna Residence, Kiawah Island,
Thomas & Denzinger, Architects

Stuart Residence, Kiawah Island, Christopher Rose, Architects

Officers and Regional Directors Of the American Institute of Architects from South Carolina

1924 - 1927
Nat Gaillard Walker
Rock Hill
Regional Director

1952 – 1954
G. Thomas Harmon
Columbia
Regional Director

1963 – 1965
William E. Freeman, Jr.
Greenville
Regional Director

1972 – 1974
William A. Carlisle
Columbia
Regional Director

1977 – 1979
H. Harold Tarleton
Greenville
Regional Director

1981 – 1983
Richard A. McGinty
Hilton Head Island
Regional Director

1986 – 1988
James Lee Thomas
Spartanburg
Regional Director

1990 – 1992
Gayland B. Witherspoon
Clemson
Regional Director

1995 – 1997
James A. Neal
Greenville
Regional Director

1999 – 2001
Thompson E. Penney
Charleston
Regional Director

2002
Thompson E. Penney
Charleston
First Vice President

2003
Thompson E. Penney
Charleston
President

 **Past Presidents Of the AIA/SC**

AIA South Carolina acknowledges with gratitude those who have served this Chapter and have been leaders of the profession of architecture in South Carolina for more than 80 years.

1913-1914
Charles C. Wilson

1915-1916
Albert W. Todd

1917-1918
E.D. Sompayrac

1919-1920
H. Olin Jones

1921-1922
N.G. Walker

1923-1924
J.D. Newcomer

1925-1927
Haskell H. Martin

1928
George E. Lafaye

1929
J.B. Urquhart

1930-1934
Albert Simons

1935-1936
Samuel Lapham

1937
Whitney Cunningham

1938-1939
H.D. Harrall

1940
G. Thomas Harmon

1941-1945
Heyward S. Singley

1946
James C. Hemphill

1947-1948
Walter F. Petty

1949
William G. Lyles

1950
C. Hardy Oliver

1951-1952
William E. Freeman, Jr.

1953
William A. Carlisle

1954
Herndon M. Fair

1955
John M. Lambert

1956
Robert I. Upshur

1957
Louis M. Wolff

1958
John M. Mitchell, Jr.

1959
A. Hugh Chapman

1960
Homer D. Blackwell

1961
William S. Dowis

1962
Ralph McPherson

1963
H. Reid Hearn, Jr.

1964
John W. Weems

1965
F. Earle Gaulden

1966
Harold J. Riddle

1967
Phelps H. Bultman

1968
Ladson D. Tankersley

1969
T.J. Bissett

1970
Frank E. Lucas

1971
Joseph L. Youn

1972
Frank D. Hemphill

1973
Richard A. McGinty

1974
H. Harold Tarleton

1975
Robert B. Cannon

1976
Kirk R. Craig

1977
Peter A. McKellar

1978
James L. Thomas

1979
Don E. Golightly

1980
W. Daniel Beaman

1981
Wrenn M. Creel

1982
Howard D. Moormann

1983
Jakie H. Lee

1984
Robert H. Kennedy, Jr.

1985
Marshall F. Clarke

1986
William T. Davis

1987
Gayland B. Witherspoon

1988
Jeffrey M. Rosenblum

1989
Sidney W. Stubbs

1990
W. Douglas Corkern

1991
James A. Neal

1992
Samuel L. McCleskey

1993
Myles T. Glick

1994
Thompson E. Penney

1995
Lynn G. Craig

1996
Charles J. Hultstrand

1997
Brooks R. Prince

1998
Thomas J. Hund

1999
Michael P. Keeshen

2000
Barbara M. Price

2001
D. Wayne Rogers

2002
Edward T. Zeigler, Jr.

2003
P. Douglas Quackenbush

2004
Mary Beth Branham

Fellows of the American Institute of Architects

Members who have made contributions of national significance to the profession of architecture are recognized and honored by membership in the institute's College of Fellows.

Charles C. Wilson, Columbia, 1913

Albert Simons, Charleston, 1934

Samuel Lampham, Jr., Charleston, 1937

Heyward S. Singley, Columbia, 1956

George Thomas Harmon, Columbia, 1957

Harlan E. McClure, Pendleton, 1962

William G. Lyles, Columbia, 1964

William E. Freeman, Jr., Greenville, 1965

Louis M. Wolfe, Columbia, 1967

Walter F. Petty, Columbia, 1968

Thomas J. Bissett, Columbia, 1972

William Carlisle, Columbia, 1973

H. Harold Tarleton, Greenville, 1980

George C. Means, Clemson, 1980

Richard A. McGinty, Hilton Head Island, 1981

Joseph L. Young, Clemson, 1982

Frank Lucas, Charleston, 1983

F. Earle Gaulden, Greenville, 1985

Kirk R. Craig, Greenville, 1986

Gayland B. Witherspoon, Pendleton, 1988

James Lee Thomas, Spartanburg, 1989

Thompson E. Penney, Charleston, 1990

Sidney W. Stubbs, Charleston, 1990

James F. Barker, Clemson, 1994

Marshall F. Clarke, Greenville, 1994

William T. Davis, Greenville, 1995

David J. Edwards, Jr., Columbia, 1995

James A. Neal, Greenville, 1997

R. Christian Schmitt, Charleston, 1999

# AIA Emeritus Members

AIA South Carolina members retired from the profession or who are above 70 years of age are considered to be members emeritus in the AIA South Carolina.

Ralph H. Aiken
Aiken Cost Consultants

David L. Bowie

Henry D. Boykin
Boykin & Munnerlyn Associates

Phelps H. Bultman

R.D. Burbank

John W. Califf, Jr.

John M. Carlisle, Jr.

A. Hugh Chapman, Jr.

Dennis B. CLark

William K. Connor

Wrenn M. Creel

Ray N. Crowe
Crowe Design

William M. Cureton

W.S. Dowis, Jr.
Dowis Associates, Inc.

David J. Edwards, Jr.

B.D. Elam

Fant, Albert R.
Fant & Fant

Charles William Fant
Fant & Fant

Harrison S. Forrester

R. Badger Gasque, Jr.

William N. Geiger, Jr.
Development Properties Inc.

Herman Christian Grube

Helmut W. Hackl

W. Edwin Hallman

Norman H. Hayes, Jr.

H.R. Hearn, Jr.

Tim S. Hilkhuijsen
Atelier Architecture, LLC

J. Thomas Hollis

A. Wynn Howell

Ephraim Hubert

Robert S. James

William J. Keenan III

Harold Dean Kent

John M. Lambert

John B. Langley

George C. Lee
G.C. Lee, AIA Architect Ret.

Peter R. Lee

Thomas W. Loosbrock

J. Harold Mack
JHM Architects, Inc.

William R. McCall,

M.C. McGarity, Jr.
McGarity Gilmore Forrester
　　Architects

Richard A. McGinty,

Leslie L. McMillan, Jr.

Michael McMillan
Architecture Consultant, Inc.

George C. Means

John M. Mitchell
Miralles Associates, Inc.

Richard D. Mitchell

James P. Morris

C. Hardy Oliver, Sr.

Johyn A. Parillo
Craig, Gaulden & Davis, Inc.

D.L. Parrott
D.L. Parrott Architect

Vito R. Pascullis
LS3P Associates Ltd.

Maynard Pearlstine

George M. Polk, Jr.
Clemson University

George L. Porcher
The Canterbury House

Samuel Rufus Putnam, Jr.

Aaron A. Rice

Charles N. Robinson

Kenneth J. Russo

Milton H. Sadler

F.W. Santillo
Santillo Group Architects

Bond R. Sedberry

James H. Small III

Charles B. Smith

James L. Tupper

Robert I. Upshur

A.R. Vanston

Leroy S. Wallace

John W. Weems, Jr.

James Duncan Wells

Malachi A. Williams
The Boudreaux Group

Gayland B. Witherspoon
McMillan Smith & Partners
　　Architects, PLLC

Joseph L. Young

Avery Wood

167

AIA Members

AIA members are licensed architects who are entitled under state law to practice architecture.

Edward Abraham

Jeffrey R. Abrams
Watson Tate Savory Architects, Inc.

Josie S. Abrams
Schmitt Sampson Walker Architects

Eric C. Aichele
LS3P Associates Ltd.

David J. Allison
Clemson University

William J. Allison
Allison Ramsey Architects, Inc.

Robert A. Almanza
Johnson & Associates, Architects

Donald J. Altman
Altman Architectural Group, LLC

John F. Anderson
Pelham Architects LLC

Raymond H. Anderson, Jr.

Robert E. Anderson
The LPA Group, Inc.

William H. Anderson

Toren N. Andersson
McMillan Smith & Partners Architects, PLLC

Danny N. Ard
Ard Wood Holcombe & Slate, Inc.

Ronald E. Ardis

Robert Dennis Ashley

Roger M. Attanasio
LS3P Associates Ltd.

John Atwater, Jr.
HP Architects, PC

Joseph A. Austin

Frank H. Bain
Neal-Prince & Partners Architects, Inc.

Charles D. Baker, Jr.
Architectural Concepts, Inc.

Don Baker
Opus, Inc.

Thomas G. Baker
TBA/SC, Inc.

Thomas S. Baldwin
Southern Management Group

Harry D. Ballard
JHM Architects, Inc.

Louis P. Batson III
Batson Architects, Inc.

Don Baus
LS3P Associates Ltd.

W. Daniel Beaman
Cummings & McCrady, Inc.

Leslie Becker
Becker Associates

Raleigh J. Beckham
The LPA Group, Inc.

Peter O. Bellows
Jacobs Engineering

David E. Benham
Neal-Prince & Partners
    Architects, Inc.

Linda Wood Berri
McKay Zorn & Associates

S.C. Berry
Carl Berry Architecture

Gregory R. Beste
Beste/Corkern Architects, PA

Kenneth M. Betsch
Design Strategies, LLC

Brian Eugene Bezilla
McMillan Smith & Partners
    Architects, PLLC

David L. Bishop
Southern Division, NAVFAC

Mary H. Bissett
Brennan Associates, Inc.

Clyde H. Blair
Thomas & Denzinger Architects

Gary J. Boehm
Glick/Boehm & Associates,
    Inc.

Glen B. Boggs II
McMillan Smith & Partners
    Architects, PLLC

Kenneth O. Bolin
LS3P Associates Ltd.

Joseph B. Bond
McMillan Smith & Partners
    Architects, PLLC

Alan O. Bornmueller

John A. Boudreaux
The Boudreaux Group

Rick L. Bousquet
Liollio Associates, Inc.

David L. Bowie

Steven K. Bowman
Jacobs Applied Technology

O. Douglas Boyce

Mary Beth Branham
Stevens & Wilkinson of SC, Inc.

James J. Brennan
Brennan Associates, Inc.

Paul A. Brickell
Brickell Architects, Inc.

Stephen H. Bridges
Wiggins & Associates, Inc.

Peggy Ann Brock
McMillan Smith & Partners
    Architects, PLLC

Ivan L. Broman
Hart Howerton

Gary W. Brown
Goforth Brown & Associates,
    Inc.

V. Stokes Browning
Browning Architects, Inc.

Terry E. Buchmann
The Boudreaux Group

James Clinton Burdett
JHS Architecture: Integrated Design, Inc.

John A. Butch

Sanford E. Byers
Byers Design Group

Richard T. Bynum, Jr.
Bynum Architecture

Jose R. Caban
Clemson University

Brian M. Campanella
Opus

Daniel L. Campbell
McMillan Smith & Partners Architects, PLLC

Paul P. Campbell
MCA Architecture, Inc.

Richard E. Campbell, Jr.

Walter M. Carns
W. Powers McElveen & Associates Inc.

Allen R. Carter

Joel Carter
Carter Architecture

Joel M. Carter
Jumper, Carter, Sease/ Architects, PA

Suzanne R. Childs
Childs Architecture, LLC

Debra McFalls Chitwood
SGM & Associates, Inc.

David W. Christine
GMK Associates, Inc.

John L. Ciccarelli, Jr.
McKellar & Associates, Inc.

Mark G. Clancy
LS3P Associates Ltd.

Richard M. Clanton
Group 3 Architecture Interiors Planning

Douglas F. Clark
Glick/Boehm & Associates, Inc.

Frank J. Clark
FJ Clark, Inc.

L. Ray Clark
Clark Architecture, Inc.

Keith M. Clarke
MCA Architecture, Inc.

William A. Clarke
CGA Facilities Services, Inc.

John C. Clayton
Clayton Design, Inc.

Steven H. Coe
Rosenblum Coe Architects, Inc.

Brian A. Coffman
Montgomery Architecture & Planning, Inc.

Donna G. Collins
University of SC

M.S. Collins
Key Collins Architecture, Inc.

Ben G. Compton
Architects BC, Inc.

Elliott Augustus Constantine
Constantine & Constantine
    Architects

Paul R. Cook
Batson Architects, Inc.

Barry M. Cooke
Jacobs Sirrine

Georgia Coundoussias
MCA Architecture, Inc.

Lawrence W. Courtney

Ana Covington Creed
Jumper, Carter, Sease/
    Architects, PA

Frederick G. Crafts
Trident Technical College

David B. Craig
Fluor Daniel

Lynn G. Craig
Clemson University

Tom Z. Crews
Tom Crews Architects, Inc.

C. Wayne Crocker
Hollis-Crocker Architects, PC

John B. Crouch, III
Cummings & McCrady, Inc.

Mary P. Schumerth Crozier
Furman University

Kevin F. Culhan
Allora, LLC

Henry D'Antonio
Goff D'Antonio Asssociates,
    Ltd.

J. Randolph Dabney
Banyan Senior Living

Sandrine Danielson
LS3P Assoicates, Ltd.

Jesse Curtis Davis, Jr.
Curt Davis & Associates, Inc.

Martin Alan Davis

Matthew J. Davis
Davis Architecture, Inc.

M. Brian Deichman
McMillan Smith & Partners
    Architects, PLLC

Hermann Denzinger
Thomas & Denzinger, Architects

J. Michael DeRienzo
J. Michael DeRienzo, AIA

John C. Derrick
MJA, Inc.

Richard J. Deskie

David Leroy Dixon
Craig, Gaulden & Davis, Inc.

J. Spencer Dixon
Neal-Prince & Partners
    Architects, Inc.

Judith Ann Dixon
Stubbs Muldrow Herin
    Architects, Inc.

Rush D. Dixon III
Stubbs Muldrow Herin
    Architects, Inc.

Dennis M. Donahue
Mitchell & Donahue Architects

Michael W. Donkle
Stewart Cooper Newell
    Architects

Stephen Thomas Dorn
DSP Architects, Inc.

Cecil M. Drakeford
Drakeford Architects

Edwin B. Drane
Town of Hilton Head Island

Frank T. Dreyer
McMillan Smith & Partners
　　Architects, PLLC

James Craig Duller
Jenkins Hancock & Sides

John G. Dumas
SE Design & Development, Inc.

David M. Dunlap
MJA, Inc.

Roy Allan Dwelley
Roy Dwelley Architects AIA

Richard R. Earl
Ellerbee Becket

Douglas B. Eason
New South Design, LLC

Allen Keith Edens

Byron M. Edwards III
LS3P Associates Ltd.

Mark S. Eggl
Design Partnership, Inc.

Lewis M. Eisenstadt
Odell Associates, Inc.

Albert H. Eleazer, Jr.
O'Neal, Inc.

Robert A. Engler

William D. Evans
Evans & Schmidt Architects

Nina M. Fair
Fair Consulting, LLC

Thomas M. Fant
Heyward Woodrum Fant
　　Associates

Paul Alfred Ferry
Jacobs Engineering

David N. Fisher
Thomas & Denzinger, Architects

John A. Fisher

William J. Fleming
Design Collaborative, Inc.

Joette R. Flora
The Boudreaux Group

Regina R. Floyd
Watson Tate Savory Architects,
Inc.

Jeff R. Fogle
Batson Architects, Inc.

Harry O. Forehand
McMillan Smith & Partners
　　Architects, PLLC

Harison S. Forrester

Marsha H. Forrester
McGarity Gilmore Forrester
　　Architects

William Furman Forrester, Jr.
Jacob Engineering

Jefferson D. Fort
Bourrough-Chapin

Douglas E. Fraser
JHS Architecture: Integrated
　　Design, Inc.

Linna J. Frederick
Frederick & Frederick Architects

Michael D. Frederick
Frederick & Frederick Architects

Allen L. Freeman
Freeman & Major

Michael M. Frick
The Boudreaux Group

Hal E. Fuller
FW Architects, Inc.

M.G. Fuller, Sr.
FW Architects, Inc.

Brooks S. Fullerton
Seamar Fullerton Hudson
　　Design, Inc.

Courtney T. Furman
Furman Architects, LLC

Robert E. Gable
Edens & Avant

H. Clayton Gandy
McMillan Smith & Partners
　　Architects, PLLC

James H. Gandy
Gandy & Associates, PA

Mark B. Garber
Mark B. Garber & Associates

Donald A. Gardner
Donald A. Gardner Architects
Inc.

Marshall Cook Gardner, Jr.
Architects BC, Inc.

Joe Albert Garrett
Lockwood Greene

Scott L. Garvin
Garvin Design Group

Michael C. Gentemann
G2 Design, LLC

Stephanie B. Gentemann
G2 Design, LLC

Robert V. Gerber
Gerber Janaskie

Ronald E. Geyer
Craig, Gaulden & Davis, Inc.

Ronald T. Gillen

Andrew Dale Gilliland
A. Dale Gilliland Architect

Thomas J. Gilmore
McGarity Gilmore Forrester
　　Architects

Myles I. Glick
Glick/Boehm & Associates,
　　Inc.

David Sullivan Glymph

R. Garey Goff
Goff D'Antonio Associates, Ltd.

Joseph E. Goforth
Goforth, Brown & Associates

Steven W. Goggans
SGA

Donald E. Golightly
Design Collaborative, Inc.

Lisa Gomperts
LS3P Associates Ltd.

Mario A. Gooden
Huff & Gooden Architects

Robert H. Goodson, Jr.
Robert Goodson & Associates

Neil W. Gordon
Herrman & Gordon Architects PA

Ronald E. Gossen II
Atelier Architecture, LLC

Richard J. Gowe
LS3P Associates Ltd.

Charles A. Graham, Jr.
Fluor Daniel

David Allen Graham
Graham Group Architecture

Steven D. Graudin
Stubbs Muldrow Herin Architects, Inc.

David K. Greer
Langley + Associates Architects, LLC

T. Ashby Gressette
Stevens & Wilkinson of SC, Inc.

Toni L. Grimes
Neal-Prince & Partners Architects, Inc.

David H. Groseclose
IDC

Derek Scott Gruner
JHS Architecture: Integrated Design, Inc.

Anna Z. Hack

William R. Halasz
William R. Halasz Architect PC

John D. Haley

David S. V. Hall
Pike McFarland Hall Associates, Inc.

Michael Hallasy
O'Neal, Inc.

Barbara L. Haller
The Boudreaux Group

James C. Hambright III
Architecture Incorporated

J. Timothy Hance
J. Timothy Hance, Architect, PA

David Eugene Hardy
O'Neal, Inc.

Kenneth E. Harkins
LS3P Associates Ltd.

Stephen G. Harrill
The LPA Group, Inc.

Sarah Wesco Harrison
Wesco Architectural, LLC

Harry C. Harritos
Clemson University

Eric Harrod
Goff D'Antonio Associates

John S. Harvell
Sarratt Associates, Inc.

Gwinn G. Harvey
McMillan Smith & Partners Architects, PLLC

James F. Harvley
Harvley & Associates

Robert E. Hawsey
Stevens & Wilkinson of SC, Inc.

Terence J. Healy
CRB Consulting Engineers, Inc.

John P. Henderson
IDC

James D. Henshaw
Stephen Herlong & Associates

Michael D. Henthorn

Stephen M. Hepler
Pegram Associates, Inc.

Samuel B. Herin
Stubbs Muldrow Herin
　　Architects, Inc.

Stephen P. Herlong
Stephen P. Herlong & Associates

Phillip Herrington
Herrington Architecture, Inc.

K. E. Herrman
Herrman & Gordon Architects
　　PA

Tim S. Hilkhuijsen
Stephen P. Herlong & Associates

Allen Tate Hilliard

Corey Hilton
Jacobs Engineering Group, Inc.

John Bell Hines
HP Architects, PC

Kevan Hoertdoerfer
Christopher Rose Architects

George M. Holcombe
Ard Wood Holcombe & Slate,
　　Inc.

Donna Holcombe-Burdette
The Highlands Group, LLC

Samuel E. Holder
Ryans, Inc.

Patrick J. Holland

Peter K. Holland
USC Construction Services

Alan M. Horne
MCA Architecture, Inc.

Martha Mitchell Howitz
Moseley Wilkins & Wood

Charles L. Hudson, Jr.
Seamar Fullerton Hudson
　　Design, Inc

Ray Huff
Huff & Gooden Architects

Charles J. Hultstrand
The Boudreaux Group

Thomas J. Hund
LS3P Associates Ltd.

Earle G. Hungerford
Pazdan-Smith Group

Robert Randall Huth
The Boudreaux Group

Alan Wayne Jackson
McKellar & Associates, Inc.

John B. Jackson
Jackson & Sims Architects

Alex C. James
SC Office of School Facilities

Michael L. Janaskie
Gerber Janaskie

Charles G. Jeffcoat
University of South Carolina

W. Barry Jenkins
JHS Architecture: Integrated
　　Design, Inc.

Ashley Kluttz Jennings
Prescon Architectural Design,
　　LLC

Robert S. Johnson
Johnson & Associates
　　　Architects, LLC

J. S. Johnston
Johnston Design Group

Albert B. Jolly, Jr.
Albert B. Jolly Jr. & Associates

Darrell Scott Jones
Kiawah Island

Gregory T. Jones
JMD Architects, Inc.

Morelle C. Jones
Tynes Associates, Inc.

Robert C. Judd
Justice Design Studio PC

Samuel D. Justice
Justice Design Studio PC

Thomas Neal Kanipe
Design Partnership Inc.

Michael E. Karamus
Michael E. Karamus Architect

John G. Karpick
Lockwood Greene

Christopher M. Karpus
McMillan Smith & Partners
　　　Architects, PLLC

Anders J. Kaufmann
Carter Goble Associates, Inc.

James T. Keane
KRA, Inc.

Michael P. Keeshen
Michael Keeshen & Associates

Ralph A. Keith
Keith Architects, Inc.

R.H. Kennedy, Jr.
GMK Associates, Inc.

Randolph Sims Key
Key Collins Architecture, Inc.

Glenn F. Keyes
Glenn Keyes Architects

G. Scott Kilgore, Sr.
Craig, Gaulden & Davis, Inc.

C. Douglas Kinard III
Clemson University

Thomas R. King

E. Thomas Kinghorn
McMillan Smith & Partners
　　　Architects, PLLC

William A. Kinninger
Fluor Inc.

Yuji Kishimoto
Clemson University

Regan E. Klein
Jacobs Engineering

Lawrence E. Kogut
GMK Associates, Inc.

Michael S. Kohn
Architects BC, Inc.

Mark A. Koll

Edward M. Krech III
O'Neal, Inc.

Michael W. Kronimus
KRA, Inc.

Thomas M. Krowka
Walsh Krowka & Associates,
　　　Inc.

Alan W. Lampert

C. Durwood Landis
Pazdan-Smith Group

David E. Langley
Langley & Associates Architects, LLC

Alice B. Lanham

Lisa M. Lanni
Pazdan-Smith Group

Thymie S. Latto
Tim Latto Architect

Daniel T. Lawrence
Daniel Lawrence, Architect

Chet G. Lawson
Fluor Daniel

Stephen K. Layne
The Boudreaux Group

J. H. Lee
Lee & Parker Architects

Jeffrey M. Lewis
LTC Associates, Inc.

Alfred A. Lindsay
Stevens & Wilkinson of SC, Inc.

Cherie A. Liollio
Liollio Associates, Inc.

Constantine D. Liollio
Liollio Associates, Inc.

Demetrios C. Liollio
Liollio Associates, Inc.

Samuel S. Logan III
LS3P Associates Ltd.

Lonnie L. Long, Jr., AIA

Lori M Long
Jumper, Carter, Sease/ Architects, PA

Randy B. Long
CBL Architects, LLC

Donald L. Love, Jr.
McMillan Smith & Partners Architects, PLLC

Robert C. Lowery
The Lowery Group, Inc.

J. G. Loyless
Jacobs Engineering

Robert T. Lyles
Stevens & Wilkinson of SC, Inc.

William Wesley Lyles, IV
LTC Associates, Inc.

C. S. Major, Jr.
Freeman & Major

Dale M. Marshall
Architrave, Inc.

Charles C. Martin III
McMillan Smith & Partners Architects, PLLC

Kay I. Mason

J. E. Matthews
James, Durant, Matthews & Shelley, Inc.

Donza H. Mattison
McMillan Smith & Partners Architects, PLLC

Perry M. Matz, Jr.
Fluor Enterprises

Prescott D. May
Neal-Prince & Partners Architects, Inc.

Stephen G. Mays
Stephen Mays Architecture

David L. McAbee
McAbee Architects, Inc.

Randall K. McClain
Signature Architects

Robert W. McClam
Robert McClam, Architect

Robert G. McCleskey
Fluor Daniel

Samuel L. McCleskey III
McCleskey & Associates PA

Frank A. McClure III
Coast Architects, Inc.

Joel J. McCreary
McCreary/Snow Architects, PA

Charles R. McCreight

Robert McDowell III

Gregory T. McFarland
Pike McFarland Hall Associates, Inc.

M.C. McGarity, Jr.
McGarity Gilmore Forrester

Scott A. McIntyre

Bentham W. McKay
McKay Zorn & Associates

Peter A. McKellar III
McKellar & Associates, Inc.

Michael E. McKelvy
Lockwood Greene

David Dean McManus, Jr.
W. Powers McElveen & Associates

Michael S. McMurphy
The Boudreaux Group

Cynthia E. Metz
Jumper, Carter, Sease/ Architects, PA

James D. Miller
Miller/Player & Associates

Jimmy E. Miller
McMillan Smith & Partners Architects, PLLC

John M. Miller
Lockwood Greene

Paul R. Miller
Miller Consulting Ltd.

Robert O. Mitchell
Jumper, Carter, Sease/ Architects, PA

Geoffrey A. Mohney
Liollio Architecture

Amanda L. Mole
Kiawah Island ARB

Adrienne Montare
Watson Tate Savory Architects, Inc.

Elizabeth L. Montgomery
Stubbs Muldrow Herin Architects, Inc.

Robert C. Montgomery
Montgomery Architecture & Planning

David R. Moore II
Craig, Gaulden & Davis, Inc.

Hank M. Moormann
H.M. Moormann Architect

Dean H. Morr
Stevens & Wilkinson of SC, Inc.

Kevin W. Morris
Design South Professionals, Inc.

S. Derrick Mozingo, Jr.
Mozingo + Wallace Architects LLP

Charles S. Muldrow
Stubbs Muldrow Herin Architects, Inc.

Sidney Allen Mullins
Christopher Rose Architects

Joseph C. Munnerlyn
Boykin & Munnerlyn Architects and Associates

J. Kelly Murphy III
J. Kelly Murphy III, AIA

Willie W. Murphy
LS3P Associates Ltd.

Paulette Myers
Thomas & Denzinger Architects

Salvatore Napolitano
McMillan Smith & Partners Architects, PLLC

David L. Narramore
Narramore Associates AIA Architects, Inc.

G. Michael Nelon
Batson Architects Inc.

Joel C. Newman
Thomas & Denzinger Architects

David Benedict Nocella
McMillan Smith & Partners Architects, PLLC

David H. Northam
University of South Carolina

Todd B. O'Dell
O'Dell Architects

James Ogden
BRZ, Inc.

John E. O'Sullivan
O'Neal, Inc.

K. L. Pace
Design Collaborative, Inc.

Frazer S. Pajak
Converse College

Matthew D. Parker

W. T. Parker, Jr.
Lee & Parker Architects

Randall Larry Parks
Miller/Player & Associates

Russell P. Parks
Odell International

Jamie A. Pattison
HOK Architects

Joseph M. Pazdan
Pazdan-Smith Group

Alfred John Peccini
Fred Peccini Architect

Steven L. Peckham
Freeman & Major

Joseph T. Pegram
Pegram Associates, Inc.

William H. Pelham
Pelham Architects, LLC

Gretchen M. Penney

Jeffrey W.B. Pettit
Craig, Gaulden & Davis, Inc.

John T. Pharis, Jr.

James E. Phillips
James E. Phillips Architects, Inc.

Joseph C. Pike
Pike McFarland Hall Associates, Inc.

John A. Pinckney
DesignStrategies LLC

John B. Pittman III
John B. Pittman III, AIA, Architect

Richard D. Pittman
Langley & Associates Architects, LLC

Bob Pitts
Hollis Crocker Architects

R. Cullen Pitts
McMillan Smith & Partners Architects, PLLC

Orville V. Player III
Miller/Player & Associates

Galen G. Plourde
Specwright Strategies

Dale H. Porath
Porath Architects

Judith D. Powell
Judith Powell Design Consultant

Scott E. Powell
Craig, Gaulden & Davis, Inc.

Garry Price
Design Elite

Brooks R. Prince III
Neal-Prince & Partners Architects, Inc.

Robert J. Probst
Robert J. Probst Architect

Joe E. Prothro
DSP Architects, Inc.

Michael T. Pry
Design Partnership Inc.

Palmer D. Quackenbush
The Boudreaux Group

Douglas Kelly Rackley
Freeman & Major

R. Wayne Ramsey, Jr.
Allison Ramsey Architects, Inc.

Charles B. Randolph

Carre Razzano

Mary C. Read
Wesco Architectural, LLC

Gordon W. Redfern
Stevens & Wilkinson of SC, Inc.

Wayne M. Reed
W. Powers McElveen & Associates, Inc.

Marian H. Reeves
Browning Architects

Todd D. Reichard
Ellerbe Becket

M. Hannah Leslie Reig

John P. Reuter
LS3P Associates Ltd.

Charles B. Rhoden, Jr.
Holmes Smith Developers, Inc.

David L. Rice
LS3P Associates Ltd.

William F. Riesberg
Riesberg Architects, LLC

Jack Rincon
Jack Rincon, Architect, PA

Thomas W. Rishforth
Fluor

Jerry W. Rives, Jr.
Jerry W. Rives, Jr., Architect

Robin Roberts
Palmetto Architecture

James S. Roberts
Roberts Design Group, Inc.

J. Y. Robinson, Jr.
KRA, Inc.

Colonel O. Rogers, Jr.
Catalyst Architects

D. Wayne Rogers
Catalyst Architects

Christopher H. Romney
McMillan Smith & Partners
    Architects, PLLC

Christopher A. Rose
Christopher Rose Architects

Jeffrey M. Rosenblum
Rosenblum Coe Architects, Inc.

Glenn H. Ross

John T. Rosser III

Michael G. Ruegamer
Group 3 Architecture Interiors
    Planning

Scott W. Rumph III
Designtec

Stephen A. Russell
Stephen Russell & Associates

Scott P. Sampson
Schmitt Sampson Walker
    Architects

Keith L. Sanders
Curt Davis & Associates

Samuel C. Sarratt
Sarratt Associates, Inc.

Valentine A. Satko
GMK Associates, Inc.

Joseph F. Saunders, Jr.
Moseley Wilkins Wood

Thomas M. Savory
Watson Tate Savory Architects,
    Inc.

Paul E. Schmid
McMillan Smith & Partners
    Architects, PLLC

Joseph D. Schmidt
Evans & Schmidt Architects

Kenneth G. Schneider, Jr.
Campbell, Schneider &
    Associates

Dennis Duane Schumm

Mark Schwerthoffer
Allora, LLC

Larry T. Sease
Jumper, Carter, Sease/
    Architects, PA

Robert M. Seel
Neal-Prince & Partners Architects, Inc.

Keith R. Seitz
Batson Architects, Inc.

Michael Shakespear
Rhodes/Dahl

William Daniel Shelley
James, Durant, Matthews & Shelley, Inc.

William Blount Shepard III
Shepard & Associates, LLC

Peter Edwin Sherratt
The Sherratt Company

Susanna S. Shiels
Pike McFarland Hall Associates

David L. Shook
Shook Associates

Randy L. Sides
JHS Architecture: Integrated Design, Inc.

Brenda C. Simmons
Batson Architects

S. Scott Simmons
Craig, Gaulden & Davis, Inc.

David M. Simpson
Enwright Associates, Inc.

Fayette L. Sims
Fluor Daniel

Walter H. Sims
Jackson & Sims Architects

Charles W. Slate
Ard Wood Holcombe & Slate, Inc.

Richard L. Sloop
Hussey Gay Bell DeYoung, Inc.

Brad Smith
Pazdan-Smith Group Architects

Bryan Thomas Smith
Donald A. Gardner Architects, Inc.

Henry J. Smith
Henry J. Smith Architects

J. Stephen Smith

Jason L. Smith
Smith Design Group of South Carolina, LLC

Rebecca M. Smith
LS3P Associates Ltd.

Ronald G. Smith
McMillan Smith & Partners Architects, PLLC

Thomas N. Smith
SMG

Deborah A. Snow
McCreary/Snow Architects, PA

Lyudmila Sobchuk
LS3P Associates Ltd.

Scott A. Sodemann
Sodemann Architects, Inc.

Rueben J. Solar
Glenn Keyes Architects

Amy E. Souder
McMillan Smith & Partners Architects, PLLC

Gregory A. Soyka
LS3P Associates Ltd.

Richard Lee Spitz
Jacobs Engineering

Michael W. Spivey
Spivey & Woods Architects, LLC

Dennis Holmes Springs

Lex W. Stapleton
Donald A. Gardner Architects, Inc.

Walter P. Stellpflug
GMK Associates, Inc.

James R. Steverson
Heaner, Inc.

Gil L. Stewart
The Ellis Group, PA

Dale Strecker
The FWA Group

Carl J. Stroud, Jr.

D. Richard Stroup
Milliken Corporation

Gable DeLorme Stubbs
Neal-Prince & Partners Architects, Inc.

Clavis LeLand Suddeth
GMK Associates

John C. Sullivan
Glick/Boehm & Associates

J. W. Summers
Summers & Associates

Charles M. Swit
Batson Architects, Inc.

Ted M. Talmage
Talmage Architects, Inc.

J. Sanders Tate
Watson Tate Savory Architects, Inc.

Allen R. Taylor
LS3P Associates Ltd.

Barry H. Taylor
The FWA Group

J. Michael Taylor
Design Partnership, Inc.

J. Weston Taylor
LTC Associates, Inc.

John F. Taylor
LTC Associates, Inc.

Pamela M. Taylor
Pamela M. Taylor Architect

Robert S. Tedford
Johnson & Associates

George E. Temple, IV
LS3P Associates Ltd.

Brian Scott Thomas
Design Partnership, Inc.

James G. Thomas
Thomas & Denzinger Architects

Jeffrey Dean Tilghman
Jenkins Hancock & Sides

Larry C. Timbes
Timbes Architectural Group

Mark L. Timbes
The Boudreaux Group

Nicholas D. Trakas

John Cobb Turk
University of South Carolina

Michael Tych
Tych & Walker Architects, LLP

Russell E. Tynes
Tynes Associates, Inc.

Stephen A. Usry
Usry Wolfe Koll Architecture, Inc.

Van Ronald B. Bergen
F.J. Clark, Inc.

Joel P. Van Dyke
Neal-Prince & Partners Architects, Inc.

Julie A. Vaughn
The FWA Group

D. Dwayne Vernon
D. Dwayne Vernon, AIA

Christopher C. Voso
McMillan Smith & Partners Architects, PLLC

Daniel W. M. Waddell
Michael Keeshen & Associates

James S. Walker
Schmitt Sampson Walker Architects

Michael C. Walker
Tych & Walker Architects, LLP

Gerald C. Wallace III
Mozingo + Wallace Architects LLP

Jerry A. Walter
Davis & Floyd, Inc.

Dennis L. Walton
Black & Veatch

Dennis S. Ward
FW Architects, Inc., AIA

Jeffrey C. Warren
Jeff Warren Architect

Marc William Warren
Jenkins Hancock & Sides

Michael S. Watson
Watson Tate Savory Architects, Inc.

Darrell W. Watts
Martin Boal Anthony & Johnson Architects

Peter E. Weisman
Peter Weisman Architect

John W. Wells

Steven A. Wells
Schmitt Sampson Walker Architects

Jerry L. Wessinger
SGA Architecture

Kevin E. Whalley
Dolphin Architects & Builders

Killough H. White III
LS3P Associates Ltd.

R. Bryan Whitely
Capital Projects Department

Dennis J. Wiehl
The LPA Group

Edgar C. Wiggins
Wiggins & Associates

James E. Wilkerson
Wilkerson Architects, LLC

R. I. Wilkins

Timothy D. Williams
Jumper Carter Sease/ Architects, PA

David A. Willoughby
Stevens & Wilkinson of SC, Inc.

Andrew L. Wilson
Glick/Boehm & Associates

Larwrence M. Wilund
Architects BC, Inc.

Gordon W. Windham
Wayne Windham Architect, PA

Lawrence Michael Witkowski
GMK Architects, Inc.

James Michael Witten
Arcadis

Allen P. Wood
Moseley Wilkins & Wood

Avery Wood
Ard Wood Holcombe & Slate, Inc.

Frederick W. Wood
Arcadis Geraghty & Miller

Lawrence H. Woodrum
Heyward Woodrum Fant & Associates

Grady L. Woods
Spivey & Woods Architects, LLC

William Frank Woods

David E. Woodward

John Phillip Works
Smith Bundy Bybee & Barnett, PC

David S. Wright
Enwright Associates

Brian T. Wurst
LS3P Associates Ltd.

David R. Yensan
Curt Davis Inc.

Louis G. Young
Louis Grey Young, AIA PC

Connie Dyer Zafiris
Coast Architects Inc.

Theodore, R. Zanders, Jr.
Carlisle Associates, Inc.

Edward T. Zeigler, Jr.
Craig, Gaulden & Davis, Inc.

Robert Ziermann
Pazdan-Smith Group

Jackson M. Zorn
McKay Zorn & Associates, PA

1993 AIA Chapter Meeting
South Carolina members who are Fellows of the AIA left to right are Gayland Witherspoon, Fritz Roth, Kirk Craig, Joe Young , Harlan McClure, Jim Thomas, Earle Gaulden and Thompson Penney

Associate AIA Members

Associcate AIA members are members without architectural license, who are employed, enrolled or participating in circumstances toward licensure; technical employees under the supervision of an architect; faculty members in a university program; or holders of a professional degree but without architectural license.

Andrea T. Abend

Channing Lamar Addis
MCA Architects

Stephen M. Aldrich
Peterson Associates

Glenn Allison
Stubbs, Muldrow Herin
    Architects

Robert D. Allison
Wesco Architectural

Kevin D. Ammons
Pegram Associates, Inc.

Scott W. Anderson
Christopher Rose Architects

Hillary B. Andren
Design South Professionals, Inc.

Marsha M. Bender
Arcadis Geraghty & Miller

Cynthia Elizabeth Benjamin
DesignStrategies LLC

Thomas Bradley Benjamin
Craig Gaulden & Davis, Inc.

Donna Bickley
Stevens & Wilkinson of S.C.,
    Inc.

Heather Kathleen Brantley
Stubbs Muldrow Herin
    Architects

Peter P. Brower
BRZ, Inc.

Kenneth J. Brown
Batson Architects, Inc.

Allen A. Buie
McMillan Smith & Partners
    Architects, PLLC

David Burt
LS3P Associates Ltd.

James M. Butler
PMH Architects

Tracy L. Cain
LS3P Associates Ltd.

Michael Evan Cantrell
Neal-Prince & Partners
    Architects, Inc.

Stephen A. Carter
Carter Goble Associates

Christopher M. Caudle
Altman Architectural Group

Christopher T. Cecil
McMillan Smith & Partners
    Architects, PLLC

Andrew M. Clark
McKellar & Assoicates

Beau Clowney
Beau Clowney Design

John Samuel Collins
A. Dale Gilliland, AIA

Richard D. Connor
Neal-Prince & Partners
    Architects, Inc.

Irene E. Constantine

Dennis Coppola
Tych & Walker Architects, LLP

A. Clemson Coyle
F.J. Clark, Inc.

George Kyser Crow
Crow Design

James H. Daniel
Craig Gaulden & Davis, Inc.

Jessie L. Daniels
A. Dale Gilliland, AIA Architect

Kevin N. Davis
McMillan Smith & Partners
    Architects, PLLC

Matt Deierlein
KRA, Inc.

Kevin James DeMark
ESA Services, Inc.

Mel L. Dias
Craig Gaulden & Davis, Inc.

William David Drennan
F.J. Clark, Inc.

Brandon K. Edwards
Johnson & Associates,
    Architects, Inc.

Michael S. Edwards
Design South Professionals, Inc.

Holly G. Esterline, Jr.
Catalyst Architects

Brian Andrew Fessler
The Boudreaux Group

April M. Fisher
Schmitt Sampson Walker
    Architects

Dennis C. Friend
Graham Group Architecture

Nicholas Gertstner, Jr.

Elizabeth Jane Gillette
Trico Engineering Consultants

Jennifer K. Gilmer
Stubbs Muldrow Herin
    Architects,   Inc.

Karen Timms Godsey
GMK Associates, Inc.

Gustavo Gonzalez-Angulo
Mozingo + Wallace Architects,
    LLP

Kenneth Gorski
PMH Associates

Jennifer Jones Gosnell
Craig Gaulden & Davis, Inc.

R. Christopher Gray

Heath Gregory
McMillan Smith & Partners
    Architects, PLLC

Carol A. Haneline
MCA Architecture, Inc.

John D. Hansen
Craig Gaulden & Davis, Inc.

William F. Harris
Allison Ramsey Architects

Turkreshaa Haynesworth
Mosely Wilkins & Wood

Marshall Lee Helena, Jr.
Altman Architectural Group

Timothy B. Hemphill
Batson Architects, Inc.

William E. Hereford III
Moseley Wilkins Wood

Franklin E. Hinson
DSP Architects, Inc.

Robert J. Hogan

Marcia Holanda
McMillan Smith & Partners
    Architects, PLLC

J. Glenn Howard
Catalyst Architects

James M. Hubbard
Pegram Associates, Inc.

P. Kenneth Huggins, Jr.
Christopher Rose Architects

Jeff Hughes

Kevin M. Hyslop
McMillan Smith & Partners
    Architects, PLL

Aaron Michael Jeffers
FJ Clark, Inc.

Glenn P. Johnson
Neal-Prince & Partners
    Architects, Inc.

Marshall Clay Jones
Jacobs Engineering Group

Elaine B. Keane
KRA, Inc.

Carmella C. Kisner
Pazdan-Smith Architects

Michael Thomas Kissam
MCA Architecture, Inc.

C. Bruce Knight
GMK Associates, Inc.

Danielle Kovach
Schmitt Sampson Walker
    Architects

Gretchen L.H. Lambert
LTC Associates

Scott A. Lambert
The Boudreaux Group

Virginia D. Lane

Stephen Shane Lather
Altman Architectural Group, LLC

Anthony T. Lawrence
Enviro AgScience, Inc.

Margaretta B. Lawrence

Carl D. Lintner
GMK Associates, Inc.

Marjorie S. Longshore
Stubbs Muldrow Herin, Architects

Bryan P. Lusk
Usry Wolfe Koll Architecture

Raphael R. Maher III
Brantley Construction

Michael J. Martinez
Neal-Prince & Partners Architects, Inc.

Christopher S. McCarthy
Christopher McCarthy Architects

William M. McCord, Jr.
GMK Associates, Inc.

Meredith Ashley McCormick

Jennifer A. McGuire
Stevens & Wilkinson of SC, Inc.

Michael Shawn McHugh
McMillan Smith & Partners Architects, PLLC

Wendy Kaye Minor
Maree Design, LLC

Jon Robert Moore II
The LPA Group, Inc.

Ana Riza Moreno
McMillan Smith & Partners Architects, PLLC

Gerlinde Mueller
Batson Architects, Inc.

Sharon A. Murray
LS3P Associates Ltd.

Nicholas Charles Nye
Timbes Architectural Group

R. Fleet Odom
Usry Wolfe Koll Architecture

Mollie Pelletier
McMillan Smith & Partners Architects, PLL

Emily Miller Peterson

Kris Phillips
McMillan Smith & Partners Architects, PLLC

Victor Pluznyk, Jr.
McCleskey & Associates

Brian Powell
The LPA Group, Inc.

John K. Powell
LTC Associates

Eddie T. Reeves
McMillan Smith & Partners
 Architects, PLLC

Charles A. Riley
LTC Associates

Mary Jo Riley
The FWA Group

Daniel Maurice Roberts
FJ Clark, Inc.

Diane Rogers
Moseley Wilkins & Wood

Priscilla Singleton
McMillan Smith & Partners
 Architects, PLLC

Megan Welborn Smith
LS3P Associates Ltd.

Thomas J. Smith, IV
Design Collaborative

Tracy H. Spake
Carolina Interiors

Phillip Benjamin Steele
Lee Nicholas Clark Patterson

Gregory L. Strickland
LS3P Associates Ltd.

Barry D. Sutton
GMK Associates, Inc.

Aleksander Tamm-Seitz
McMillan Smith & Partners
 Architects, PLLC

Monte Glen Taylor
Agra Simons, Inc.

Michael F. Thomas
Justice Planning Associates, Inc.

Larry Thompson
LCM Design Group, Inc.

Jeffrey K. Tiddy
Craig Gaulden & Davis, Inc.

Emily R. Tinkler
Neal-Prince & Partners
 Architects, Inc.

Gregory G. Tucker
Colliers Keenan, Inc.

Michael Anthony Vaccaro
KRA, Inc.

Debra L. Viviano
McMillan Smith & Partners
 Architects, PLLC

Cameron Wilson
LS3P Associates, Ltd.

W. Steve Wilson
Neal-Prince & Partners
 Architects, Inc.

Brian Wolf

Stephanie Elizabeth Wood
Stevens & Wilkinson of SC, Inc.

Professional Affiliate Members

Professionals affiliated with design

Allen R. Beckett
New England Financial

Robbie Boland
Keystone Block Group/Keystone Carolinas

F. Drucilla Brookshire
Guy White & Associates

Linda S. Love
Professional Practice Insurance Brokers, Inc.

Carole Reams
PGT Industries

AIA/SC Staff

Angela B. Taylor
Executive Vice President

Tracey B. Waltz
Executive Diretor

Miriam W. Payne
Administrative Assistant

Selected Bibliography

Anonymous, *The American Institute of Architects College of Fellows History and Directory* (privately printed, 2000).

John M. Bryan, *An Architectural History of the South Carolina College, 1801-1855* (Columbia: University of South Carolina Press, 1976.

_____, *America's First Architect, Robert Mills* (New York: Princeton Architectural Press, 2001).

_____, *Robert Mills, Architect* (Washington, D.C.: American Institute of Architects, 1989).

_____, *Creating the South Carolina State House* (Columbia: University of South Carolina Press, 1999).

William J. Heiser, *Lockwood Greene, 1958-1968, Another Period in the History of an Engineering Business* (privately printed, 1970).

James F. O'Gorman, Jeffery A. Cohen, George E. Thomas, G. Holmes Perkins, *Drawing Toward Building, Philadelphia Architectural Graphics, 1732-1986* (Philadelphia: University of Pennsylvania Press, 1986).

Walter F. Petty, *Architectural Practice in South Carolina, 1913-1963* (Columbia: South Carolina Chapter of the American Institute of Architects, 1963).

Alfred Coxe Prime, compiler, *The Arts & Crafts in Philadelphia, Maryland and South Carolina, 1786-1800, Part II* (New York: Da Capo, 1969).

Jonathan H. Poston, *The Buildings of Charleston, a Guide to the City's Architecture* (Columbia: University of South Carolina, 1997).

Mills Lane, *Architecture of the Old South, South Carolina* (Savannah: Beehive Press, 1997).

Albert Rains, chairman. *With Heritage so Rich* (New York: Random House, 1966).

Beatrice St. Julien Ravenel, *Architects of Charleston* (Charleston: Carolina Art Association, 1945).

Anna Wells Rutledge, *Artists in the Life of Charleston through Colony and State from Restoration to Reconstruction* (Columbia: University of South Carolina Press, 1980).

Albert Simons and Samuel Lapham, *The Early Architecture of Charleston* (Columbia: University of South Carolina Press, 1970).

John E. Wells and Robert E. Dalton, *The South Carolina Architects, 1885-1935, a Biographical Dictionary* (Richmond: New South Architectural Press, 1992).